D1284603

Creating a
New Civility

BLISS INSTITUTE SERIES

Bliss Institute Series
John C. Green, Editor

Joy Marsella, *Creating a New Civility*

William L. Hershey, *Quick & Quotable: Columns from Washington, 1985-1997*

Jerry Austin, *True Tales from the Campaign Trail: Stories Only Political Consultants Can Tell*

William L. Hershey and John C. Green, *Mr. Chairman: The Life and Times of Ray C. Bliss*

Douglas M. Brattebo, Tom Lansford, Jack Covarrubias, and Robert J. Pauly Jr., editors, *Culture, Rhetoric, and Voting: The Presidential Election of 2012*

Douglas M. Brattebo, Tom Lansford, and Jack Covarrubias, editors, *A Transformation in American National Politics: The Presidential Election of 2012*

Daniel J. Coffey, John C. Green, David B. Cohen, and Stephen C. Brooks, *Buckeye Battleground: Ohio, Campaigns, and Elections in the Twenty-First Century*

Lee Leonard, *A Columnist's View of Capitol Square: Ohio Politics and Government, 1969–2005*

Abe Zaidan, with John C. Green, *Portraits of Power: Ohio and National Politics, 1964–2004*

Creating a New Civility

Joy Marsella

UNIVERSITY OF AKRON PRESS
AKRON, OHIO

All Material Copyright © 2020 by The University of Akron Press

All rights reserved · First Edition 2020 · Manufactured in the United States of America.

All inquiries and permission requests should be addressed to the Publisher, The University of Akron Press, Akron, Ohio 44325-1703.

ISBN: 978-1-629221-23-6 (paper)
ISBN: 978-1-629221-88-5 (ePDF)
ISBN: 978-1-629221-87-8 (ePub)

A catalog record for this title is available from the Library of Congress.

∞ The paper used in this publication meets the minimum requirements of ANSI / NISO Z39.48–1992 (Permanence of Paper).

Cover design: Amy Freels
Cover illustration: Susan Panning

Creating a New Civility was designed and typeset in Mrs. Eaves and Mr. Eaves, with Univers display by Amy Freels. *Creating a New Civility* was printed on sixty-pound white and bound by Bookmasters of Ashland, Ohio.

Produced in conjunction with the University of Akron Affordable Learning Initiative. More information is available at www.uakron.edu/affordablelearning/

To Judy Hunter, identical twin and soulmate, who helped me create civility by believing in my project and providing daily encouragement, engaging in hundreds of conversations about the nature of civility, offering thoughtful responses and asking critical questions, crafting my words for cohesion and clarity, and, most important, helping coax an emerging framework into a paradigm.

Contents

Acknowledgments

Thank you, Laura and Gianna, daughters dear, for cheering me on at every stage of this work and for unbounded confidence that I would envision what full humanity means and how it would help individuals and our society flourish. My sister Margaret, sons-in-law Dave and Eric, and seven grandchildren—Taylor, Connor, Calista, Miranda, Alora, Annabelle, and Harrison—chimed in with their support too.

Thank you, Susan Panning, graphic designer, who encouraged me at all stages of the project, especially at its beginning, and created visualizations that capture the essence of the paradigm's five processes.

This book would not have been possible without the help of the librarians of the Fairlawn-Bath Branch of the Akron Public Library System. My thanks especially to the public service assistants who looked in nooks and crannies of SearchOhio to find the books whose authors helped me understand and redefine civility for this day and age.

Thank you to Dr. John C. Green, Distinguished Professor of Political Science, director of the Ray C. Bliss Institute for Applied Politics at The University of Akron, and chief advocate for its Greater Akron Civility Center. Professor Green saw promise in my manuscript and put it in the hands of board members at The University of Akron Press. I am grateful to the staff at the Press: to Jon Miller for his sound advice, to Amy Freels for her lovely book design, to Julie Gammon for her enthusiastic promotion of my book, and especially to Thea Ledendecker, for her extraordinary care and professionalism as she partnered with me to make my text as clear and readable as possible.

Key Concepts

Awareness—the goal of practicing mindfulness; a sense of presence arrived at through consistent meditative practices; noticing what is happening in the moment and accepting of it; a positive, even happy acknowledgement of one's humanity, as expressed in each moment of now.

Bodyheartmindsoul—a word crunch that captures the totality and complexity of our being, the recognition and accommodation of the simultaneity enabling the creation of civility.

Citizens—those who embody civility and, in doing so, contribute to the communities in which they live, making them vital and strong; those who takes civic responsibilities seriously—first and foremost, studying issues and candidates, voting and, furthermore, ensuring that other eligible citizens get to vote.

Civility—a combination of belief and behavior that allows a community —and, by extension a country—to thrive, the combination underpinned by a commitment to democracy, and, in the United States, to the support and sustenance of our Constitution and its amendments and of our citizenry. Unfortunately, the word *civility* is also sometimes used as a tool of oppression, with the assumption of superiority being that others need fixing, or brought into line, or trained; the "object of the "civilizing" is assumed to be lesser.

Common Cause—the hard work of citizens finding best ways to make communities fair and just for the people who inhabit them—to level the playing field so all can rise and thrive, none at the expense of another; the efforts carried out with sensitivity to the circumstances and history of those involved; the effort of cooperatively coordinating efforts with others also at work in the community.

Common Good—the coordinated effort of citizens and citizen groups to provide homes, energy, place, space, education, money, laws—or some combination thereof—to address a community's issues, bringing citizens together in the process; the lovely sense of gratification that comes to those who benefit from and carry out community care, defined broadly here.

Common Ground—the agreed-upon points of departure in the search for solutions to problems or for carrying out a project; a shared concern for, even love for, a place or purpose or people that serves as motivation to make improvements, to create beauty or to offer a moral demonstrate of caring.

Compassion—a sympathetic interest in and for a community's citizens; a quality manifested in active interest in and interaction with others; implies a willingness and intention to connect with and care for those whose lives touch ours, immediately or remotely; manifested as the opposite of hate, suggesting that, in creating civility, all of Earth citizens are understood as fully human.

Consubstantiation—a quality described by Kenneth Burke as "being with" another to the extent that there is an overlapping or coming together of our substances, of mind and matter, used here as an ultimate kind of caring—and that which is necessary in the search for reason and the quest for civility.

Developing Empathy—caring for people and by extension their places; consistent with the idea that individual acts of civility, the civility of our governmental institutions, and our contemporary civilization as such, flourishes on positive emotions and diminishes in negative ones.

Fairness—the goal of interrogating identity, in which we as citizens strive to be free of prejudice, and balance our own interests, needs and feelings with those of the other, taking into account the present circumstances and history of others, and treating them without prejudice, in a manner addressing past discrimination; acts as fulcrum from which actions, processes, and goals spring.

Full Humanity—the apogee of civility marked by consideration of others, for which we as citizens strive and which we so desire; the feeling of benevolence we recognize for both ourselves and others, used here for those times, approaching a state of grace, when we have met our five goals of fairness, awareness, harmony, compassion, and insight—individually and/or collectively; that which eventuates from authentic practice of mindfulness.

Harmony—the goal of listening anew, achieved when we really hear what others are saying, when we truly "get" another's needs and desires, supporting and helping them emotionally and actually, and, by extension, helping all of us live fully, fairly, and accountably.

Insight—the goal of reasoning well; the inner nature of civility dynamics, that of understanding identity, practicing civility, listening anew, and developing empathy; that power that is achieved through an integration of all of our actions with their various processes—put more directly, insight grows from fairness, awareness, harmony, and compassion.

Interdependence of Us All—the assumption that we live in a global village in which all of us are equal, fully human, culturally intelligent, and deserving of respect; the recognition that our actions have consequences that emanate locally and quickly, and reverberate far beyond us; a realization that results from soulful meditative practice.

Interrogating Identity—a private, honest review of qualities that mark and shape our behavior, called *markers* here; thinking deeply about how these markers intersect and act together as a force for prejudice and/or positivity; the honesty eliciting discomfort, because we recognize our own incivilities or those of family and friends, or because we have not acted to correct them, or to call out others who are culpable.

Listening Anew—Immersing ourselves in another's words in new ways, allowing us to say, "I hear you!"; cultivated through identity interrogation and mindfulness practice, and essential to the development of empathy.

Other—(n.) someone or some group that we see as different from us in basic and distinctive ways; (v.) to separate oneself from or cast disdain on those different from us, in prejudicial or hateful ways. We have likely been on both the giving and receiving ends of othering.

Paradigm—a framework by which a citizen can live a life imbued with civility; humanistic ways of being, mental and behavioral habits that serve as morally driven principles to bring about civility; its five components building on one another logically, holistically, and recursively; based on an understanding of one's life in a local community as vital to a strong democracy, mindful always of global ramifications of citizen choices and behaviors, individually and collectively.

Practicing Mindfulness—the relaxed and kind attention to our bodies, hearts, minds, and souls through consistent meditation that focuses on breathing and body scans, recognizing that (in)civilities are often bodily based and hormonally driven by fight-or-flight instincts or variations of them, creating the necessity of being in touch with our bodies.

Privilege—a special right or advantage assigned to those in power because of wealth, heritage, gender, or race; those without privilege are all too often relegated to a lesser position in which they are subject to ill treatment; the tradition of privilege often so inherent that those who hold it are unable to see it (or resist seeing it)—a behavior referred to as *white fragility*.

Process—a philosophical tradition devoted to becoming and to change; the underpinning practice of the paradigm for a new civility with its five actions building one on another and yet always available for review, in any order necessary; this practice advanced through journaling and discussions in civility circles.

Reasoning Well—entertaining the complex acts and situations of civility dynamics, drawing on good thinking from great minds across the ages, acknowledging the who, what, where, when, how, why of any situation, and considering how what came before structures what is happening now; a balanced process essential to fair governance at all levels—and to creating civility.

Introduction

Civility is best understood as a community-building impulse or mood that requires the fulfillment of three criteria (numbers added for emphasis):

    1. the full humanity of the self and others;

    2. the recognition of interdependence with the other;

    3. and the desire to make common cause with the other.

    Courtesy is part of such a civility, but only insofar as it does not serve to relegate certain groups of individuals to second-class status. Justice is compatible with such a civility, but only insofar as it is not an absolute justice that insists on the priority of principles to human beings.
—Adam McClellan

Welcome to our civility journey.

As you can see from the epigraph, we are defining civility broadly, in a way that encompasses the richness and complexity of life in the new millennium. Our definition promises transformation and is based on three basic and beautiful concepts—full humanity, interdependence of us all, and common cause. Thank you, Adam McClellan, for defining these three concepts that work so well for our purposes here.

Complex as these concepts are, they are at the heart of our personal lives, our communities small and large, and the public institutions within them. When realized, they offer a better life, immediately and locally, in the ongoing moments of each day. Interestingly, the practices reverberate, from one person to another, from community to community, and so on. This reverberance carries the potential for change.

These three concepts, which seem remote and possibly even beyond reach, are with us the moment we are born. Our humanity is shaped through the caregiving that sustains us in the early years. We grow through interdependent relationships. We learn what interdependence means through managing the give-and-take of family and social life and learning how our own lives compare and contrast with others. Through these interactions, we understand possibilities for common ground, and learn to make common cause for common good. This same dynamic, when fully realized, allows our communities and the public institutions within them to thrive as well.

When all goes well? When fully realized? Learning give-and-take? Full humanity when I'm just managing to get along? Interdependence when my own life is so demanding? Finding common ground? Making common cause? Really?

Yes, really. We move through our days anyway, seeking ways to make our life better.

Why not seek full humanity, elusive as it may seem? Why not make the best of the interdependence that is a fundamental reality? Why not see life through the lens of the other in order to find ways to make life better for all, in order to make common cause? In all practicality, the other are there; ironically, we are their others. No getting around it.

I promise a profound and fulfilling adventure, one that allows you to make your voice heard, that moves with the times, and that offers a new social vision that will heighten the experience. Our explorations begin personally, always with an eye to how they are revealed publicly. There is boundary-crossing, from the interiority of identity analysis to the exteriority of behavior, from the personal to the public, from private individual to public citizen.

Like any personal growth program, the more diligence and commitment we bring to the activities, the more insight we gain and opportunities we create. To enlighten our exploration, I invite you as readers to accompany us—good thinkers, scholars, and researchers—whose insights add richness to our own emerging theory and practice of civility. Altogether, we create a vocabulary that allows us to talk about a new civility, to understand its complexities, and to study the way it is manifested in our lives.

We grow intellectually and interpersonally. A program with such promise needs a stable foundation in the rich thinking of philosophers, scholars, researchers, thinkers, and activists—past and present. This book provides that foundation. We build a theory and practice of civility pertinent to our own lives' staying power.

We develop an understanding of point of view, an identity "lens," through which we can better interpret people and public events—local, state, national, and beyond. We examine the hows and whys of our relationships, especially with people quite different from us, our *other(s)*.

We act, in ways small and large, to help things along, to sort through complexities, and to contribute solutions. This action takes effort and stick-to-it-iveness, as any self-help or self-improvement program does. Committing to the new civility asks us to examine the prejudices and the hatreds that keep us from realizing our full humanity in order to see if we can put an end to them to find common cause. This last sentence is worth rereading, for it is the crux of our undertaking.

Our personal transformation offers promise for public transformation. Civility theorist Lawrence Cahoone tells us that civility transformation occurs through contact with those around us in our neighborhood. He writes that "civil society is primarily local. That is, the most fundamental form of civil society is what in contemporary social terms we would call the *neighborhood*."[1] We will create civility where we live.

The new civility addresses civic action and social change, following the "do unto others" moral code that is at the heart of most religions and of civil societies. Its social and ethical foundation has potential to enrich our lives and to change the communities in which we live.

These explorations are not a recipe that guarantees success. Rather, they offer a set of good practices that will likely lead to civility if they are adopted. Think in the largest scale possible, knowing that keeping peace in your heart and in your family is a step toward keeping peace in our world's family.

A New Civility Paradigm

[C]ivility is not just good manners at Grammy's house or good citizenship in the polis. It may even be the central, unenforceable bond which makes community possible in our pluralistic world.
—Leroy S. Rouner

By undertaking this journey, we are breathing life into a new civility. Our journey will culminate in a new way of being for us as citizens. The paradigm for a new civility is laid out below.

A *paradigm* is a model or framework that offers a way of thinking about an area of thought, usually a broad one. Thinking in terms of a paradigm offers a way to understand what structures the thought and behavior of those who operate within it. Paradigm shifts are said to occur when major ways of thinking of an area or discipline change and those who inhabit the field change their behaviors accordingly. A paradigm shift opens up new possibilities for seeing the world within the specialty.

The term is most often applied to scientific fields, but in my own professional life I witnessed a shift in our understanding of how writing works and how it is best taught. Specialists began thinking in terms of writing as process—that is, how it is produced—rather than in terms of writing as product only and analyzing it as such. Suddenly new ways of helping our writing students opened up, because as teachers we could help them through drafting, revising—again and again if necessary—and finally editing their texts, a process that we saw as recursive, or repeated at any stage as necessary to get at a satisfactory written product. This shift prompted teachers to become writers, to see themselves as writers also, and to write along with their students, thus changing their way of being in the classroom. My intellectual understanding of how writing works changed my behavior. This simplification of what is a revolutionary dynamic allows you to see how I became a disciple of teaching the art and craft of writing as process, of how I became a disciple of process itself, and of how I came to understand process as a philosophy.

As you can see, I am bringing the emphasis on process to our effort here after living the civil life. The notion of paradigm allows us to think broadly of what constitutes civility, how we have thought about it in the past, how we think about it now, and what we might do if we were to shift those ways of thinking and behaving. We would hold onto what is valid and fold it into a new conceptualization. We would be thinking big, not just focusing on the moment itself but rather on a framework, or model that would allow civility to more certainly emerge, whatever the situation.

The graphic lays out the paradigm's components and gives an overview of our quest—its processes, actions, and goals. I use the word *paradigm* intentionally to capture the momentousness of our undertaking. The framework moves civility study into our hands, as ordinary people who comprise a country's citizenhood. At the same time, it provides a kind of architecture that allows an individual to engage at a level beyond the personal, one that

PARADIGM FOR A NEW CIVILITY

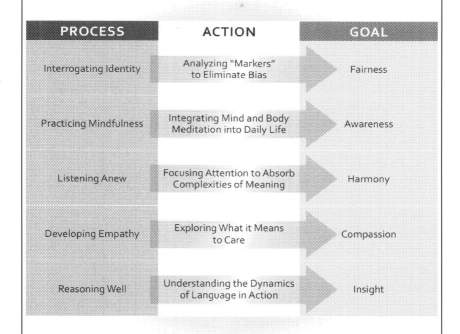

PROCESS	ACTION	GOAL
Interrogating Identity	Analyzing "Markers" to Eliminate Bias	Fairness
Practicing Mindfulness	Integrating Mind and Body Meditation into Daily Life	Awareness
Listening Anew	Focusing Attention to Absorb Complexities of Meaning	Harmony
Developing Empathy	Exploring What it Means to Care	Compassion
Reasoning Well	Understanding the Dynamics of Language in Action	Insight

TOWARD
... INTERDEPENDENCE OF US ALL...
... COMMON GROUND, COMMON CAUSE, COMMON GOOD...
... FULL HUMANITY...

Illustration by Susan Panning

has political and social ramifications. Civility in this rendering is tied to place, yet our components are universal. Our definition assumes we all have a fundamental worth and dignity, described here as *full humanity*; we relate to one another in terms of community, described as *interdependence of us all*; and given that we do so, we want to make *common cause* with one another. The individual is not denied; indeed, the individual is front and center, yet not alone. Ultimately, the individual is linked to community.

This new paradigm sets ambitious goals. Yet we only have to take our journey one step at a time to understand the concepts and behaviors involved in each of our five processes and to see how they fit together and build on one another to create a dynamic whole—resulting in a new civility that allows us to address life at the beginning of a new millennium, accounting for its always-dynamic change. We are developing a philosophy of living centered in civility.

Usually we think of civility as a concept that is already out there, one that we contribute to by being civil and courteous. Or we think of civility as a remote abstraction that has little to do with our day-to-day lives. Here we create a new civility through five processes that teach fairness, awareness, harmony, compassion, and insight. These five processes are imbued with life flow, allowing us to think through how we behave privately and how we interact publicly, always with the realization that we are citizens after all, no matter what group(s) we are in at the moment. Their flow is outward, as human life always is. Making common cause is what we must do for our communities, small and large, not only to survive, but also to thrive.

The concepts of community and neighborhood are foundational to the paradigm and the actions within it. Indeed, we can truly think of the world as a community, given the technological breakthroughs of the new millennium that allow us to communicate instantaneously with different people throughout the world. The paradigm promotes a new way of thinking about ourselves as world citizens. We are in the process of redefining what it means to live in a community in this technological age. Thinking globally and acting locally takes on a new urgency now that our understanding of community is becoming more flexible, yet at the same time less intact—given that online groups and even foreign entities can influence a community's thinking, and thus their behavior, through their influence on social media.

What will be our foundation? Our platform? Our paradigm? Why not civility?

Resolve to Reach an Ideal

*It falls to each of us to be those anxious, jealous guardians of our democracy, to embrace the joy-
ous task we've been given to continually try to improve this great nation of ours. Because for all
our outward differences, we all share the same proud title: Citizen.*
—**Barack Obama**

I'm certain that you have already noticed my idealism. Why not hold
out for an idea that has such promise for us and for our worlds, small and
large, in the drama of everyday life, and in a quest for finding common
ground therein?

This quest is worth undertaking: worth the hard work; worth the
endless repetition of saying "We are citizen"; worth the intriguing explorations of what *civility* and *citizen* mean as those concepts play out in the
drama of everyday life and of local and national politics; worth the
patience of explaining the ideal.

Let us not be embarrassed to claim the ideal. We would not think of
berating someone who tries to be the best athlete, dancer, artist, chef,
journalist, or even the best politician. Indeed, we celebrate them. Why be
reluctant to embrace citizen ideal and celebrate civility?

It only takes one person at a time to embrace civility and to invite
others to join this interesting process of moral accountability.

Mark Edmundson, in *Self and Soul: A Defense of Ideals*, asks: What has happened to the ideal in our society? He describes three ideal selves—the hero,
the saint, and the thinker.[2] He points out that heroes possess courage, as
did the warrior Achilles in Homer's *Iliad*; saints show compassion, as did
Jesus, Buddha, and Confucius; thinkers practice contemplation, as did
Plato, Aristotle, and Emerson.

What has happened to the ideal? I propose that we add a fourth to
Edmundson's three examples—that of citizen—one who exemplifies the
qualities laid out in our new civility paradigm and meets its challenges.

Hero. Saint. Thinker. Citizen. The citizen will need hero/saint/thinker
qualities in finding common ground. Like the hero/saint/thinker, we as
citizens realize that

- we have a choice in how we act;

- creating civility is a choice;

- the choice is a deliberate, intentional decision to be responsible to our families and our communities; and

- our choice involves a broad, generous, and inclusive perspective, one that shows no fear of unfamiliar faces, places, or spaces that support different social, political, or religious customs. In this sense, we resist partisanship.

I invite you to hold out for that fourth ideal, citizen, who, in facing the challenges of daily life, acts accountably, holding in mind that the good that they do in their neighborhood will reverberate.

Hold Civility in Your Hands

The graphic personalizes our quest. It shows the processes spelled out on the thumb and fingers of our left hand, and the goals associated with them on our right, as follows:

- Interrogating Identity = Fairness

- Practicing Mindfulness = Awareness

- Listening Anew = Harmony

- Developing Empathy = Compassion

- Reasoning Well = Insight

In a meditative moment, position the fingertips of both hands together so that the five processes and goals connect, so that identity interrogation connects with fairness, mindfulness practice with awareness, and so on. Fingers intertwined, think of what your fingertips sense, what your hands hold, what is pressed together between them—the possibility of civility, as realized by a deep understanding of your identity; your body, heart, mind, and soul; your surroundings; your relationships; and your ability to reason your way through life challenges. I encourage you to return to this gesture again and again throughout our journey as a way to center yourself in the wonder that is civility.

We will be able, when we face differences, to hold the image of civility in our hands in order to review if, when, and where we are culpable. Life in our global village requires that we ask this question. Honestly, our planet, and life on it, is too fragile not to.

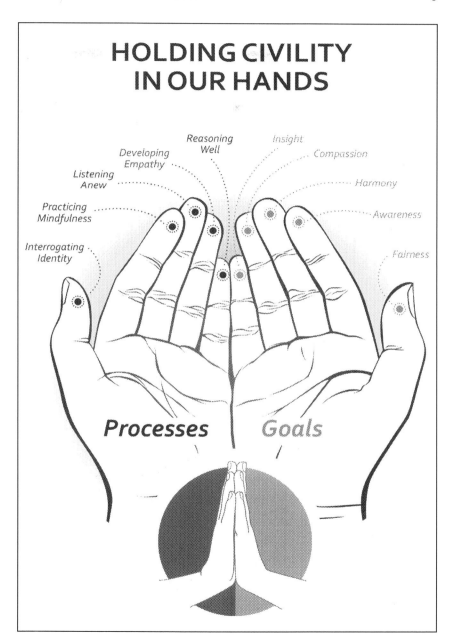

Illustration by Susan Panning

To return to the imagery of holding civility in our hands, when we open and extend our hands, we gesture to full humanity. The gesture aligns us with love and caring, and, in doing so, we resist hate and prejudice. Our gesture is systemic and therefore integrative. Through its repetition, we have the pleasure—and sometimes the challenge—of discovering the *other* (one of a different gender, race, religion, politics, ethnicity, age, place, class, education, and ability) with an attitude of respect. We entertain difference, and the beliefs and practices that accompany it, be they racial, religious, or political. We take interest in them as part of our developing civility intelligence. Moreover, we study them and interrogate our less-than-civil past behaviors in order to change—to play our parts in bringing about fairness for all. We are comfortable doing this: our principles are secular, yet consistent with the loving-kindness doctrine common to most religions.

In the emerging moments of now within which we achieve these goals, we sense our potential, achieving a full-humanity high. Imagine feeling one with humankind and our universe. It's possible. We just don't usually think in these terms—so large-scale, positive, and optimistic.

Through our explorations, we come to sense the deep structure of civility, which we will see more clearly as we delve into it.[3] Just as our heroes were courageous, our saints compassionate, and our thinkers contemplative, we as citizens will engage civility and accept the challenges and changes necessary to claim the ideal. We will learn not only the conceptual but also the particular; indeed, our accountability is in the particular.

Our singular self-examination holds a modicum of humility. Our endeavor, such as it is—flawed often in the trying, two steps forward and one back—will bring ourselves and others to the ideal of citizen, to an embodiment of civility.

We who embody civility are doers. The wonder of civility is that its resonances are potentially limitless, and much of it is so easy—the smile, a nod of acknowledgement, and an others-first deference. Its beauty is in its potential—why so many of us want it so much, and have so much faith in it, even in a time when many feel that it is under siege on the national stage, in social media, on our streets, and in public places where we go to relax. Just as society has wanted and needed heroes, saints, and thinkers, it now asks for citizens who embody civility.

I invite you to undertake two practices as you journey toward civility—write your thinking down and talk to others about it. I formalize these practices in *Creating A New Civility* as keeping a journal and participating in a civility circle. These practices are time-tested by writers and thinkers as ways to advance understanding and inspire creativity.

As you read, jot down ideas that stand out, and as you complete the exercises at the end of each chapter, journal about any impressions or reflections that come to mind. As you move forward in your civility journey, periodically revisit your notes to see how your ideas may have grown and changed.

You will find yourself inclined to talk about your insights with others, so I suggest you organize four or five acquaintances with whom you can regularly share your emerging understandings. You will want the circle setting to be safe and open enough to welcome personal explanations yet organized enough to invite inspired, even daring commentary from all participants. I offer suggestions for discussion throughout *Creating A New Civility*.

Civility is, after all, a social activity. Keeping track of your thinking and engaging in discussion about it are authentic, enjoyable ways to integrate civility into your life journey as citizen.

A Word on Courtesy and Manners

I'm often told of the discourtesies that people experience in everyday life, and of how they long for the respect that goes along with their concept of common decency. They wish for my book to address the fundamental disrespect that many feel is so prevalent in our society.

I believe that courtesy comes with civility. The two go hand in hand. Still, there are moments when courtesy guidelines in and of themselves are relevant, and I list sources on my website, www.civilitydynamics.com, that cover etiquette and general rules for considerate conduct. Several of the civility definitions there explain how the relationships between courtesy and civility evolved.[4]

As I explain *Creating a New Civility* to interested people, I get four responses. "Well, we certainly need that book!" or, skeptically, "What are you going to say—'be nice?'" Others ask what civility actually is beyond courtesy and good manners. Still others believe my project is totally beyond realization: "Good luck with that!" The implication seems to be that there is little hope for civility in our society, that the project is too large and unwieldy, and that our population, partisan as it is, will be unreceptive.

I think otherwise. I invite you to join me on this most intriguing journey, with its attraction for connections—from practical application to nearly mystical nuance (when civility wavelengths connect us to others in ways we couldn't have imagined) to the satisfaction of trying for an ideal.

This is self-improvement, self-help, how-to—writ large. This is due diligence for civility. The journey improves us in amazingly rich and wonderful ways, and it has the potential, through us, to make our communities healthier and happier.

Think of bringing the aura of citizen ideal to our lives—an idea that is expansive, not selfish; open to possibility rather than a done deal; that moves away from me-first, self-serving scramble of dates and deadlines to the soulful understanding of those with whom we interact. Focus your daydreaming here. Talk a friend or two into sharing the journey, joining a civility circle, making opportunities for reflection richer. Take your time on your journey: you may want to read through the work quickly to get a sense of its whole; then you can study each of the processes individually, moving through them thoughtfully so that you can truly absorb the principles therein, so that at the end of your study you will truly embody civility. The learning is calming and satisfying, and once the practice becomes habit, instantaneous recall applies—mind-muscle memory kicks in when we need the calm of mindful awareness, and of insights that help us understand how our identity and behavior is and has been shaped.

Why Undertake this Journey to Civility?

Never doubt that a small group of thoughtful, committed citizens can change the world. Indeed,
it is the only thing that ever has.
—Unknown, commonly attributed to Margaret Mead

Because we do not live alone. From our very first moments we relied on a nurturing relationship with a mother, father, or caregiver. We have needed others to survive. We live in interaction with humanity, with those like us, and different from us.

Because, as the center of our personal universe, we can make changes within it. Whether civility lives in our universe depends in large part on us. We can teach by setting an example. We can plant ideas. Whether or not civility blossoms depends on innumerable people in innumerable settings interacting with a sense of dignity.

Because we are attracted to the equanimity of a civil life. Our reasons may be personal, spiritual, religious, or political—all are ways to approach human dignity and common good. Nothing in our civility journey contradicts these thoughtful approaches to the common good; in fact, the ideas here are consonant with them. Our new civility abhors discrimination and asks for inclusivity.

Because of the precariousness of all kinds of human, animal, and plant life on our planet today. So much hangs in the balance. We no longer want to accept the destructive, violent behavior that too often characterizes life in our global village.

Because, in the words of a "pay it forward" stranger, "There's not a lot of civility around these days." I was in line for my soy latte at Starbucks when the man in front of me covered my bill. A rush of humanity flowed through me, transferred from him, in that momentary act of kindness. Overwhelmed, I thanked him, told him I was writing a book on civility, signified in his very act.

Because, cliché aside, we want to make this world a better place. On a personal level, if we recognize our own dignity, and extend it to others, we create, for the moment, a common good. The civility idea is planted in and around us.

Because, in the words of David Brooks, "There is no way to repair national distrust without repairing individual relationships one by one. This is where national renewal begins."[5]

Because we can make a difference in the here and now, in the moment by moment of our lives. I love Margaret Mead's message about the power of an individual to shape change. Adopting civility ideal, with its moral center, we can change the tenor of our world, in the moment by moment of individual ways and days.

Because, at the beginning of a new millennium, the time is right. The political order is tenuous, here and abroad. Our country holds its breath and prays for civility as the current administration carries out its plans; the conflicts in the Middle East seem always to be with us; human tragedies, here and abroad, seen through heartrending photographs and courageous journalism, are viewable on our cellphones instantaneously; and the planet is made even more fragile through environmental damage wrought by the world's most developed countries.

Let us have faith in the future and resolve to connect the new millennium to civility. For the good of the world, and of its citizens (including ourselves), let us don the civility mantle and think in the imagery of the ideal. Civility as full humanity emanates from us, extends to others, enacts a positive life force, for the good of where we are, in this place, in the here and now, in the moment by moment of our lives. In doing so, it gives our lives a moral center of gravity and a new social vision.

A commitment pledge below will help to sustain you through this process. I model our pledge below on Julia Cameron's contract in *The Artist's Way: A Spiritual Path to Higher Creativity*. I suggest you sign the commitment, copy it, and place it prominently as a reminder to keep your pledge.

You are following a community-building impulse with moral and civic integrity at its center. I wish you well in your endeavor.

A New Civility Commitment

I, _____, understand that I am undertaking
    an intensive, guided encounter
    to reach for the full humanity of citizen ideal.
    I commit to seeing my way through five processes
    in order to gain an understanding of the new civility,
    so that I can bring about civil change
    in the places I inhabit and with people I encounter.
    "Full humanity, interdependence of us all, and common cause"
    becomes my mantra.

I, _____, further understand that these processes
    will raise issues and emotions for myself and others to deal with.

I, _____, commit to caring for myself and others,
    and creating civil situations that build civil communities.

Signature_____ Date _____

Process #1
Interrogating Identity—
Toward Fairness

In undertaking this first process, we are embracing an ideal, a role that is transformative and different from society's often rude, self-centered, contentious, partisan, recriminatory, and sometimes, hateful behavior. Quite a line of adjectives! Ones that roll trippingly on my tongue, alas, because I see the behaviors too often.

In moving away from such incivilities, we join those who are deeply committed to the full humanity of us all, who are aware of our interdependence with the other, and who desire to make common cause with others.

We wish to create a powerful shift in America's—indeed, the world's— collective consciousness, a shift that leads to respect for all. We wish to create a new civility.

Here in process #1, we ask a lot of questions—we are carrying out an interrogation, after all! Through our questioning, we analyze four qualities—I call them *markers*—that shape our identity and that are at the center of the discussion of civility: gender, race, politics, and religion.[1]

Ultimately, we will uncover something of how they operate in life's contentious situations to shape incivilities.

Write Your Identity Story—for Civility's Sake

In his thoughtful bestseller *Between the World and Me*, Ta-Nehisi Coates explains how his grandmother responds to him when he misbehaves. She asks him to interrogate his behavior. I go to this passage because her goals are similar to ours, as you will see. Coates writes:

> When I was in trouble at school (which was quite often), she would make me write about it. The writing had to answer a series of questions: Why did I feel the need to talk at the same time as my teacher? Why did I not believe that my teacher was entitled to respect? How would I want someone to behave while I was talking? What would I do the next time I felt the urge to talk to my friends during a lesson?[2]

It is the particularity of these questions that helps Coates get to a deep sense of his behavior, to understand the context in which it occurred, to probe his relationship to his teacher, and to see himself in the context of his class—for the purpose of greater self-understanding.

Coates repeats the interrogation process with his son. Notice the lesson Coates draws from it, as it is relevant here. The emphasis is mine.

> I have given you these same assignments. I gave them to you not because I thought they would curb your behavior—they certainly did not curb mine—but because these were the earliest acts of interrogation, of drawing myself into consciousness. *Your grandmother was not teaching me how to behave in class.* **She was teaching me how to ruthlessly interrogate the subject that elicited the most sympathy and rationalizing—myself.** *Here was the lesson:* **I was not innocent.** *My impulses were not filled with unfailing virtue. And feeling that I was as human as anyone, this must be true for other humans. If I was not innocent, then they were not innocent. Could this mix of motivation affect the stories they tell? The cities they built? The country they claimed as given to them by God?*[3]

Here Coates plays a major role in helping Americans understand their history of antiblackness. He tells his son, "This is your county, this is your world, this is your body, and you must find some way to live within the all of it."[4] In our search for a new civility, we are answering his call to action.

Like Coates, we must find some way to live in our world, and our bodies—in civility. We will adopt his interrogation process in order to see where we are "not innocent."

We are consciousness-raising here: we are capturing both the amorphousness and the particulars of our identity and examining them. Just as Jesus, Buddha, Emerson, and Thoreau undertook self-study as they carried out their significant work, so must we. We too are disciples, just as they were—in our case, our commitment takes us into the deep structure of civility.

Here we scan four pillars of our identity, in the way an MRI scans sections of our body, and in a deeply thoughtful, meditative state. We will implicitly ask, in each of the four marker categories, as Coates has: Where am I "not innocent"? When we know our culpabilities and where our prejudices and biases are, we can do something about them.

Our inherent tendency is to guard against or repress these reactions. The identity investigation will help bring them into our felt experience, that is, into the visceral responses that the emotional connection gives rise to, into the reactivity of strong emotion, of love, or even hate.

We have a choice.

Each of us carries a unique heritage, an *identity provenance*. In the quest for a new civility, we go to the pillars of that heritage. We want to examine our provenance, address what is revealed, reexperience it through conversation and writing, tease out the implicit, and make it explicit.

Our analysis may rattle our comfort zones, in its big-picture yet personal look at getting along in our world. I think of this as the good hurt of a massage, when the therapist presses hot spots to alleviate the soreness in order to heal our bodies.

We are unique. Each of our identity markers is unlike any of the other 7.6 billion people in our global village,[5] of the other 326,000,000 in the United States.

Miraculously, each of us is singular.

This amazing realization helps us understand the complexities of human identity, and of the difficulties of getting along harmoniously. We can enumerate the complexities: 7,600,000,000 (estimated world population) x 10 (for our purposes, the traits that mark our identity) = 76,000,000,000. All of us, in our complexity, have 76 billion different identity markers among us. This equation gives us pause: the complexity of identity within the relative handful of people with whom we interact is incredible.

We do not have to deal directly with a billion complexities in our daily lives, although sometimes it feels as if we do. But we do indirectly, in that those who live across the world are part of our global village, and their actions, sometimes individually (Osama bin Laden, Kim Jong Un), or as a group (ISIS, Ku Klux Klan), have an instant impact on us as we watch the news. This realization is easy to become numb to, or ignore, as we go about our lives in our limited geographical sphere, sometimes far from tensions arising in other parts of the world, and with our own set of pressing problems.

In terms of our identity investigation, women, minorities, those of lower social class—any person, really, on the margins instead of the mainstream—can suffer the indignity of challenges to their identity. On a personal level, we feel this pain in our role as parents when children challenge our authority, or, more significantly, when our children's autonomy is challenged or abused. On a national level, activists are challenging those who hold and have held power and acted unfairly—sometimes unlawfully—calling them out for their injustices. Think of the #MeToo movement and Black Lives Matter.

Grappling with Point of View

You and I are having a conversation of sorts—you reading my reasoning, thinking about it, and talking back to its ideas. You are noticing differences in our points of view. My identity is revealed through my choices and voice. I can only guess at your identity. The fact that you found your way to this book reveals a shared interest, always a starting point for a relationship.

Not acknowledging our points of view is like denying our selfhood. Point of view is powerful, something not easily changed, and challenging it raises its hackles. Even as we profess open-mindedness, we hold a point of view, which will eventually be revealed, as mine is here.

Further, our subject, civility, is personal, and our choices about it are driven by some combination of hereditary instinct, innate impulse, momentary emotion, practical experience, and education—all of which are highly personal and construct our points of view.

I pledge to write, keeping in mind that my collective audience will have a range of viewpoints, none aligned directly with mine. I will do my best to avoid a strident, righteous tone. I will write with an eye to the qualities of our goals—fairness, awareness, harmony, compassion, and insight—as I guide your journey to the new civility.

Coming to a new point of view involves embracing new landscapes, so our journey metaphor is appropriate.

I ask you to meet me halfway, and to stay with me when disagreement or disappointment occurs. These moments are at the crux of any journey, and especially with a civility journey—staying with a contentious conversation so that disagreements have a possibility of resolution, so that compromises and counteroffers can be heard, so that common cause can be found. I understand the emotional upheavals that deeply held disagreements cause. We have to grapple with them, to make them less devastating to our psyche. So, we will invite reason, history, and relationships into our conversation. I will turn to scholars who help us along in critical thinking. I will ask you to track your own thinking and experience, to be willing to broaden your horizons, to be self-critical, in a positive way. For (in)civility is not entirely personal. It has very public ramifications, as we are seeing now on our national scene.

You've already discovered something of my point of view. I write about my identity below, noticing that which impinges on (in)civility.

Disclosure #1: Generally speaking, I admit to a liberal predisposition that has been shaped by my mother's reading of life events; my now ex-husband's secular humanism and his exploration and acceptance of new cultures and their people, impulses I shared as his spouse; thirty-five years learning about the different cultural traditions of Hawai'i's people; thirty years in liberal academia teaching students from Hawai'i's islands and from East and South Asia and Polynesia. I learned to see the world by learning about the experiences of others.

Disclosure #2: At seventy-eight, I know I have lived a good life. I have lived in (white) privilege. My voice was not suppressed. I suffered from neither deprivation nor fear and from little anxiety. I worked hard. I always had nourishing food to eat, fresh from farm to table in my formative years; a large, loving family; clean, safe households in which to live; good health; nice homes in "good" neighborhoods; nice clothes, and the self-indulgence of really lovely ones after I started earning my own income; good schools and teachers, undergraduate education supported by my parents, and graduate education that earned me faculty status at a university I could be proud of; plenty of friends; a decent amount of money; and opportunities to travel some of the world.

You may well be thinking that, of course she can go on about the civil life, given the fortunate life she has lived. No poverty. No unemployment. No crime. No discrimination. How can she ever understand? How can she see the world through my eyes?

I will try to do so. Civility asks that I try. Our new civility paradigm offers a way to do so.

Civility asks that we take the trouble to learn about other people's circumstances and their history. Civility asks that we educate ourselves about the political, sociological, and economic ways of our world. Civility asks that we learn about egregious discrimination involving gender and race. Civility asks that we try to understand why people hate and hurt. Civility asks us to act on our understandings, on behalf of those who have been wronged. I have tried to do so.

That said, I don't believe we should make way for any old argument just because it is out there in our world. We look at its merit, especially how it advances civility in our world (more about reasoning in Process #5).

I also believe in some basic truths. One is that human life is and has always involved a continual process of change. Another is that humans are adventurous; they have traveled, intermarried, and populated our Earth— out of pure spirit of exploration and also out of need for better, safer places to live. Those processes are bound to continue. People have always searched for places to live that would make life better for them. We dwell in our points of view. No doubt about it. But we resolve here not to be bedeviled by them. We will work to change when we believe our points of view are not in concordance with civility.

Here in our identity interrogation, we assert "Know thyself" and ask, "Who am I?" We interrogate ourselves to get at the deep structure of our identity, to get at complexities such as early memories, learned responses, and shaping experiences. Most importantly, the process of these interrogations allows us to get at insights that stick, that carry us through tension and tragedy, that involve our whole being in order to be manifested in civil behavior. The graphic gives of visual summary of this process.

IDENTITY IS...

GENDERED • RACIAL • RELIGIOUS • POLITICAL

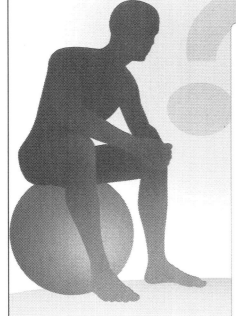

*For the sake of civility,
I ask myself,*

"Who am I?"

My identity heritage

As for Gender?_____

As for Race?_____

As for Religion? _____

As for Politics?_____

**Necessary Transformations
Headed for fairness**

_____

_____

_____

_____

_____

*Away from prejudice, bias, and
hatred or fear of others, to citizen*

Illustration by Susan Panning.

Identity Questions and Civility Activism

In the language of postmodernism, we will deconstruct our identity, examining each marker one at a time. Aiming for civility transformation, and in the tradition of Ta-Nehisi Coates's grandmother, we ask three broad questions. You can make notes in the Journaling Prompts page at the end of each section or in your civility journal. Our journaling here will be more pointed than the purely personal journaling you may have carried out in the past. The revelations are then available to you for further exploration in civility circle discussions, which gives you an opportunity to advance your thinking even further, at which point you may wish to return to your journal once again. Trust me, once you engage the questions below, they will resonate in your life experiences.

1. *Who am I, in my understanding, and exemplification of, [insert marker]?*

We answer as we see ourselves, as clearly as we can, this deep and penetrating question. We are looking at our racial experiences as they have unfolded in our lives, as we understand them on reflection. How, for example, does gender, race, religion, or politics structure our interactions? Our goal is to become so familiar with our experience of the marker under consideration that we can instantaneously see how we love and hate as we move through our days. Like Coates, we are looking to see where we are "not innocent."

Dig deeply here. Peel away layers, looking at prejudicial moments, to get at the core of each of the markers as we see and feel them in our being.

What are my experiences of othering, of being othered, and of getting to equanimity—fairness, impartiality, stability, and composure—in the treatment of others?

I use the word in distinctive ways: as a noun it means someone who is different from or opposite to oneself; as a verb, it means to separate yourself from or cast distain on someone who is different from you, perhaps in intolerable, prejudicial, or hateful ways.

2. *How have I othered (treated others with prejudice)? How have I been othered (been a victim of prejudice)?*

Your examples will reveal stories that go to the issue of difference. In each case, what happened? Who was involved? What was the setting? What motivated the exchange? In what ways was [insert marker—for example, race] at play? What emotions were evoked? How did your body feel? How was the moment resolved, if it was? What is your take on the experience now that some time has passed?

On the other hand, when and how have I treated others with generosity and helped others to find fairness, impartiality, and equity? Through such actions, civility is born.

This question set allows you to look at settings small and large, those riven with dissension, anger, prejudice, even hate.

3. Finally, and critically important: How might I move my insights to actions in order to participate in the transformation to civility?

What are possibilities for personal action? Of measuring the need for belonging against the courage to stand alone?

What are possibilities for public action? For activism? For stepping out of your own groups and for getting to know someone different from you?

Answering this set of questions gives us a frame of reference for understanding ourselves and others. This frame gives us a vocabulary and a way to analyze prejudice, how it develops, how it is manifested, and how it can be overcome—in ourselves first, and then, thoughtfully, with others.

Equally important, this interrogation allows us to avoid the partisanship that is stifling the very basic operations of democracy, as witnessed by (in) action in our legislative bodies: we are keeping an open mind about ourselves, we are thinking for ourselves, examining our heritage, and not attaching ourselves to the hatred and prejudice so often associated with partisanship.

At the conclusion of the discussion of each marker, I offer you an opportunity to write out first thoughts, which you can continue in your journal and compare with members of your civility circle. I include questions to prime your thinking for action in support of civility.

Writing down aspects of identity, and their repercussions for bias and prejudice, or for loving and hating, concretizes them and makes them available for further thought and revision. We can track our thinking as it evolves through examination of our written word. That quality allows us to come to some understanding of our identity, and to change its accompanying behaviors.

I invite you to begin your own identity narrative—in the name of civility. In doing so, you internalize the process so you can help others understand how identity is pivotal to civility.

Interrogating Identity: Sex and Gender—Toward Fairness

Welcome to identity boot camp. Let us begin with a fundamental assumption, one that is implicit in the Introduction and that we make explicit here: we have the capacity for change. This is the assumption behind all the self-improvement classes we undertake. In yoga classes, we look for renewal. In nutrition classes, we nourish our bodies. In foreign language classes, we expand our linguistic horizons. In identity boot camp, we face up to who we have been and are. When our history shows us failing to create civility, we strive to change. We want to create a new civility.

Making a change is intellectual and behavioral work. Doing so is difficult enough to result in emotional and mental fatigue, if not exhaustion.

Our goal here is to acknowledge, respect, and treat lawfully those whose gender identity is different from our own. We are looking at how our gendered identity has led us to love or to hate, to inclusivity or discrimination, or to full humanity or incivility.

Vocabulary lessons first. *Sex* refers to the classification of biological differences assigned at birth, as realized in our reproductive organs. *Gender identity* is defined as a "person's perceptions and experience of their own gender. Gender identities are complicated, and they can be binary (man and woman, male and female, masculine and feminine) or nonbinary. A person's gender identity may or may not align with the gender as assigned to them at birth based on their sex characteristics or chromosomes."[6]

Following contemporary usage, we will use *gendered* as an adjective in two ways in order to reflect:

- "the behavioral, cultural, or psychological traits typically associated with one sex," as in gendered language; or

- "the experience, prejudices, or orientations of one sex more than the other," as in gender differences or stereotypical gender roles.[7]

We will use *LGBTQ+* as an initialized umbrella term that recognizes various choices for expression of gender identity and sexual orientation (L for lesbian, G for gay, B for bisexual, T for transgender, Q for queer or questioning, and + for the many other gendered identities such as intersexual, asexual, gender nonconforming, nonbinary, gender fluid, and cisgender, and for making certain that no one is excluded from the community). So that my language usage here reflects our nonsexist impulse, I have silently corrected all sexist language in the passages I quote.

Let us recognize, thankfully, that we are living in a new legal era that is beginning to recognize rights of LGBTQ+ citizens; living in full humanity, our goal is to live in community with each other without discrimination. We can only trust the esteemed judges of our justice system to sort out the issues as pertinent cases come before them.

Not willing to ask you to do something I don't, I begin with a list of my gendered roles. As you read, think about how your roles compare and contrast with mine. I warn you—member of the Silent Generation as I am—the list is long and reflects the attitudes and choices of the era in which I was born and reared, which may be quite different from your own. Mine is gendered female. I organize mine in chronological order, as follows:

> little girl with Raggedy Ann and Andy dolls that twinsie and I shared, blocks, utensils from the kitchen that we played with between mother's feet;
>
> older sister to five other siblings, each relationship different one from the other, diaper changes, laundry, food prep, and lots of cuddling and cooing and teaching;
>
> farm girl with activities before and after school, and in summers (no trips to the pool to play with the kids from the boulevard) and at the same time a lush garden that fed us, and farm roads and woods to explore;
>
> friend to girls and boys in high school yet there was no boyfriend;
>
> off to college, at mother's insistence and with father's initial resistance (even though my high school counselor scheduled me into secretarial classes thinking my parents wouldn't be able to afford college);
>
> diligent student with mostly male professors (I count six women among my bachelor's, master's, and doctoral programs);

lover to the man I eventually married;

wife for fifty years, absolutely faithful, opportunities foregone;

mother of two daughters, unlike many men at that time, my husband never once complained about having daughters instead of sons;

teacher for three years, following one of the few options appropriate for women at the time I entered college in 1959, and following an aunt who was the first college-educated woman in our family;

professor in a male-dominated profession for thirty years, a career that took me through a nontenured instructorship, to a tenure-track position that allowed me to rise through the ranks at the same time I earned a PhD in American Studies with a specialty in American literature, ultimately to be tenured in a Department of English with publication of my book on Louisa May Alcott's short stories for children;

daughter-in-law with dependent in-laws, and a live-in mother-in-law for many years (disclosure: her caregiving eased my own career as well as my husband's);

friend to wonderful women I know from the ten different places I have called home;

a disciple of second-wave feminism in my mothering, teaching, and being;

grandmother of seven—three girls and a boy, the first born twenty-two years ago, plus three more I inherited recently from a blended marriage;

straight and cisgender, my expression of sexuality restrained, perhaps suppressed by self and circumstances;

now a writer who is in the rare territory of making decisions based only on my own needs and desires, which, I can assure you after all this time, takes some courage.

What a journey! Marked in so many ways by the eras I have lived through. Your own list will reflect the time and places you have lived in and the people you have lived with.

Now, it is your turn to take up your journal and to write your own list of roles. We all have so much in common even if we have different

gendered identities, given the variety of cultures and subcultures here in our own country and abroad.

Who Am I? Interrogating Your Gendered Roles

This set of questions (which also work for race, politics, and religion) asks that you look in the mirror and face yourself and your heritage. Boot camp rules say you cannot look away, even if it brings up uncomfortable emotions. When this happens, square your shoulders and say—as you would in any other training class—"I can do this. I can do better."

As our ultimate goal in this process is fairness, we ask basic questions: "Was I treated fairly?" and "Did I treat others fairly?" The questions below are extensions of those above, shaped for our gender analysis. I lay them out here in this first interrogation to help you with deep analysis of your gendered sense of self. Given practice here, you will be able to shape responses to questions for race, religion, and politics on your own.

1. *Shaping your sense of self. How did each of the roles you mentioned in the listing activity above shape your sense of self as female or male? In your home? At school? In workplace(s)? In leisure settings? From childhood to adulthood?*

It is helpful to ponder—how did you "learn" your gender identity—what we are calling your gendered sense of self?

How did the gendered behavior of those around you influence you?

How did your schooling, your friendships, and your role models influence your gendered sense of self?

Have you felt secure and safe in your sexual or gender identity— why or why not, when and where? Here you will address the ease or discomfort with which you accepted this identity, and what decisions you made as a result of those feelings and responses. Here you will address whether you have either suffered abuse, aided and abetted abuse, or were directly responsible for it. We note that abuse moves beyond the physical to include the emotional that includes derogation, name-calling, bullying, and a denial of selfhood.

Have you been comfortable in and with your assigned gender roles? How so? Why or why not? Answering these questions will inevitably get at whether you identify with a specific gendered role or move fluidly between and among these categories. These are significant questions that get to heart of your very being.

Expressed in the most general way possible, I ask you to think through how your gendered experience of selfhood allowed—or did not allow—your humanity to flourish.

2. *Bias and prejudice. What role have they played in your gendered experiences?*

Let us differentiate between bias and prejudice:

Bias—"an inclination of temperament or outlook" that is "personal and unreasoned," or an instance of such treatment;

Prejudice—"a preconceived judgment or opinion formed without just grounds" and not based on reason or experience, or an instance of such treatment.[8]

The differences are nuanced. Bias is more general, while prejudice goes to the specific. Neither is necessarily reasonable, but prejudice goes to a judgment or behavior that has no grounds, and is therefore discriminatory, sometimes with legal implications.

In what ways, if any, have bias and prejudice reared their ugly heads and influenced your life? Did the acts of such amount to abuse of any kind?

Once again, it is useful to pull out your journal and write about particular acts of discrimination you have faced. Describe how the particulars of the situation have impacted your sense of self.

What happened? Who did what to whom? Under what circumstances? In what setting? How was the event a violation of selfhood? How were you hurt by it? Did the violation have an impact that went beyond you? Did others come to your aid, or were you left to deal with the violation on your own? Were you ever able to figure out why the violation occurred? Was there a satisfactory resolution?

Have you been a perpetrator of sexual discrimination in the form of bias, prejudice, or abuse? In this case of perpetrator, try to get at motivating behavior. In addition to calling out the harm you may have done to others, describe the harm that came to your own sense of self, your own sense of morality, as a result of this behavior. Ask yourself "Why?" Did strong emotions, possibly of fear, distaste, or dislike underpin the prejudice or bias? If you were in a position of power, did you take these emotions as an excuse to demean or harm others? How did you come to this prejudice?

Have you played a role as observer or bystander, as one who aided a victim, as one who abetted the perpetrator, or as one who brought about resolution or healing? Think through the impact of that role on your gendered psyche.

In considering these questions, notice how our personal lives are impacted by our larger society with its various groups that hold their own biases—very evident in the political scene, such as white Evangelicals and white supremacists. "Who am I?" is related to place certainly, and to a moment in time absolutely. And so on.

3. *Gendered identity and civility. How does my gendered identity allow full humanity?*

Finally, how have these experiences, taken as a whole, shaped your point of view on questions of gender identity? Your own? Others'? On related legal issues? On how these issues make their way into—or intersect with—race, politics, and religion? On your potential for civility? So much to think about.

Suppose you think of the accumulated experiences described so far as part of your identity provenance, the part that deals with sex/ gender/ LGBTQ+. *Provenance* in this case deals with where you came from and what has been.

Now let us think of what will be—moving away from provenance to reformation. We are, after all, creating a new civility paradigm, a new framework for our personal identity. We will braid in three other parts of our identity provenance in the sections on race, religion, and politics to follow.

Finally, ask yourself: what kind of model do I wish to be—or what examples do I want to set—for my family and friends and community? Am I where I want to be in my thinking and living? Are there further transformations I can undertake in the life I have yet to live?

How can I use my experiences and insights to bring about societal change that leads to greater civility? Can I use my identity understanding to help create a more just and civil world?

Chronicling our gendered roles requires courageous thinking. Personally, I find myself revising my gender narrative regularly, whenever insights come to me, when I venture into new arenas, or when I undertake a project that requires deep thought, as I have in writing this book. Once you engage your gender identity, you will be continually thinking about it and revising it as you do so.

The three question sets above are meant to help you gain insight and to suggest a course of action. The probing nature of the questions can cause discomfort, yet the challenging work of any kind of transformation rarely occurs without deep personal introspection and engagement with ourselves, our beliefs and past practices, and our family heritage. It is through such a coming to terms with self and situation that behavior changes. Keeping a journal is a comforting, private way to begin. Seeing the answers to these questions written down, for review, concretizes your thinking, and makes it available for revision. Participation in a civility circle furthers that endeavor. The processes bring about change.

A Gender Identity Action Plan

We often hesitate to act because we don't want to disrupt a pleasant setting or rattle comfort zones. Or we realize that we might suffer ostracism if our social activism goes against shared prejudices. We acknowledge the complexity in the force of change—the traditions, the resistance, the emotions. Such is our angst on the slow march to eliminate gender discrimination, prejudice, and bias.

However, with firm resolve and the courage of our convictions, we can set priorities, think about what is most important to us (given life experience and given the lives we wish for our children and grandchildren), and go to work on the most pressing issues.

The issue of sexual harassment is the center of our national psyche, with revelations coming to a head over Harvey Weinstein's horrific predation and over three-hundred Catholic priests in Pennsylvania who abused more than a thousand children over several decades. What kind of moral culture allows such atrocities to happen and to be covered up? The #MeToo Movement brought to light the actions of actors, legislators, doctors, directors of respected publications, and those who turned a blind eye. Many of these people fell into ignominy, where they belong. Activists are also advocating for factory workers, food servers, and janitors, especially those on night shifts, who can more easily be victimized.

Society seems less apt to allow those who hold positions of power to get away with sexual harassment and predation simply because of their status, President Trump's behavior notwithstanding. I can only conclude that political partisanship, a distorted sense of nationalism, and a longing for someone whom they thought would shake up the system overrode voters' concern for his objectification of women.

Time will tell how President Trump's appointments to the Supreme Court shape the destiny of Roe v. Wade, which goes to the subject of abortion and women's right to choose. The point of view that I bring to this discussion is that the right to decide belongs only to each woman, in each circumstance. Perhaps no other issue is more strongly gendered than this one, which goes to a woman's very identity and subsequent life. I believe that failure to understand this position is a failure to grasp the significance of point of view and gender identity. It is sobering to bring this section to conclusion with discussion of this very significant issue. Yet the right to choose is a critical gender identity issue. I understand that there will be those who disagree with me. What this book teaches is that we disagree agreeably—and reasonably.

As I was in the early stages of preparing this book, the Supreme Court made momentous decisions on same-sex marriage that influenced gender perceptions from the moment it was rendered. The slow march of progress will continue as the court hears challenges to its decision, the results of which will further shape basic issues of gender politics.

Planning for Change

If you've done the writing and thinking called for, you have just completed an intellectual boot camp on gender identity. You've faced the hard work of telling the truth on issues that, in the past, may have been hidden and ignored, not addressed with straightforwardness and with the intention of inclusion. You are entertaining the ideas here with an open-mindedness that others around you might not share. Now you have a framework for bringing those who resist into the discussion. What to do next, knowing progress will be slow? The suggestions below also work for change under the markers of race, religion, and politics.

1. Set an example. Be brave. Have faith. Change will come. We are seeing ourselves not just in terms of manners and behaviors but in terms of one part of our very identity, an identity that is worthy of citizen, an identity that is thoughtfully centered in civility. Keep in mind past leaders who had a hand in bringing the gender conversation to the better place it is now. There is so much more to do. We will see that it is done.

2. Take action locally. Pitch in to ongoing efforts that are consistent with your personal insights. Think in terms of reformation.

3. Keep up with the issues and let the local and national conversation inform your behavior—to some extent.

4. Realize, though, the real power is close at hand where the hard work is being done, where we know people, and where we can trust and draw on our personal experience. This work will be more satisfactory because it is personal. We will be emotionally connected with others who are working toward similar ends.

5. We are, after all, thinking of civility not as a state of being but as an action plan, as laid out in our new civility paradigm. We are connecting our personal lives with the larger human condition.

Let us review what we have accomplished: we examined our gendered identity and looked at our experiences through the lens of fairness, understanding when we achieved it and when we did not.

We are clearer now than we were before on how our gender identity has been marked through experience. We will use that knowledge to inform our intention to live in full humanity, aware of the interdependence of us all, desiring to make common cause—in this case for gender equity. In achieving this, we will be living in civility, with courtesy, in the name of justice for individuals everywhere.

And the conversation will continue.

Journaling Prompts: Gender Identity

Full Humanity—Interdependence of Us All—Common Ground for Common Cause

- *Who am I as a [insert gender identity]? How have gendered choices and experiences influenced my core being?*

- *How have I othered?* How have I treated those whose gender identity is different from mine with prejudice or without acknowledging them or including them in my world? How have I discriminated against those of the opposite sex with a microaggression, or in ways that are even more hurtful?

- *How have I been treated as an other?* How have I been treated with prejudice, with neglect, and so on, in ways related to my sexual or gender identity? Have I suffered sexual discrimination, harassment, or abuse?

    ○ Notice here ways in which you dealt with or resisted sexual abuse or discrimination, treated others with fairness and generosity, pushing yourself and others to inclusivity and therefore civility.

How might I move my insights on gender to actions on behalf of civility? How have I already done so?

Interrogating Identity: Race—Toward Fairness

My definition of a racist idea is a simple one: it is any concept that regards one racial group as inferior or superior to another racial group in any way.
—Ibram X. Kendi

We are about to interrogate our racial identity—looking for fairness in the treatment of all races on our road to full humanity.

We will have reached full humanity when we can acknowledge that there is only one human race, a position endorsed by the American Anthropological Association. (Note that anthropology is "a field of knowledge dedicated to making the world safe for cultural differences."[9])

Indeed, the AAA position paper on race states that

Evidence from analysis of genetics (e.g. DNA) indicates that most physical variation, about 94%, lies *within* so-called "racial groups." Conventional geographic "racial" groupings differ from one another only in about 6% of their genes. *This means that there is greater variation within "racial" groups than between them.* In neighboring populations there is much overlapping of genes and their phenotypic (physical) expressions. Throughout history whenever different groups have come into contact, they have interbred. The continued sharing of genetic materials has maintained all of human-kind as a single species (emphasis mine).[10]

However, very recent studies show that all human beings are even more closely related in their genetic makeup, lending the AAA statement even more credibility. We are all genetically very, very similar. Responding to a recent controversy over human genetic variation, leading anthropologists Alan Goodman and Marcy Darnovsky, along with thirty-one other signatories, affirm that "[r]ace is a social grouping. Genetically, there is only one human race."[11] We recognize that not all anthropologists hold this view. Yet knowing of this position in and of itself, knowing of a small genetic difference among races, and knowing there is hugely more difference among races than between them—these facts argue for tolerance.

The AAA position informs our discussion of civility: when we use the concept of race, we need to study and remember how the concept has been shaped by history, science, and past usage. Really, our interrogations are a way of raising our consciousness, not just to the personal, but to the public and historical ways each marker has been handled over time.

I applaud the work of geneticists such as David Reich, whose research is changing our understanding of human genetics. I join the scholars of AAA who strive for "more nonracist and accurate ways of representing the diversity of our population." In our study of race, we seek to understand how the classification of race weaves itself "into the cultural and political fabric of the United States." We too wish to transcend and replace these classifications with "more nonracist and accurate ways of representing the diversity of the US population."[12]

In the meantime, we position our discussion under the rubric of race, holding in mind the contestations around the term. America has a shameful history of racial hatred and discrimination, beginning with the awful treatment of Native Americans that began in the colonial years—Thomas Jefferson held slaves even as he composed the Declaration of Independence and contributed to writing our Constitution. This treatment continued through the dreadful Trail of Tears, involving the dislocation and slaughter of so many, and their relocation on reservations, some of which have barely arable land. The practice of slavery was also unconscionable, ingrained as an accepted way of life for so long and by so many, with so many lives ravaged in its years of practice. We must also bow our heads in shame over our treatment of the Chinese workers who built our railroads, of the internment of Japanese Americans in WWII, and now our treatment of refugees and asylum seekers from Central America. Our creation of a new civility has to acknowledge and reckon with this history that sees people of color through the lens of extreme prejudice. This is a pivotal calling, given that we claim, indeed cherish, the interdependence of us all.

One hundred fifty years after the war that "ended" slavery, our American society still does not treat black people with equality, to say nothing of newcomers of different races. America needs a reckoning of these gross incivilities, and our search for civility is a contribution to that reckoning. Racists have subjugated and killed too many people because of their hate.

Our laws help define discriminatory behavior. Courts are deciding how to interpret racist laws in light of our constitution; our legislators—when they can overcome the obstruction of partisanship—try to refine those laws so that they are fairer to all (n.b. they were unable to do so during all of President Obama's eight years, and the partisanship has worsened under President Trump, so that legislation itself is stymied). Our churches work toward similar ends within the structures of their dogma, although still too many religious leaders continue to discriminate against other races (and genders). Enlightened civic and nonprofit and social groups address social justice, and so do individual citizens—through marches, protests, and town hall meetings—in their quest for civility.

The dissension over race goes to the issue of power—who holds it and how it is wielded. As such, power raises the issue of subjugation—the temptation of the powerful to bring the less powerful under control. As such, racial challenges intersect with social class and with poverty, due to laws and customs that are defined by or tinged in antiblackness.

Strife rages in our cities because of such discrimination. Law enforcement is a critical point, it being well documented that police stop people of color for various minor infractions more often than people who are white. A *Guardian* article found that in 2016, 1091 people were fatally shot by police in the United States; 169 of them were unarmed.[13] Black and brown children typically get "the talk"—special lessons from parents on how to conduct themselves if stopped by the police. The problem of police brutality toward people of color is one of the gravest incivilities of contemporary American life.

If we are aware of family or personal history that impinges on this issue of racial injustice—either from the point of view of those with advantage or disadvantage—we want to examine it. In our interrogation process, we are, as always, examining our emotionality and reactivity. In particular, we explore what triggers our incivilities, our discriminatory words and acts, our prejudicial thinking that ends in dismissal and hatred.

If your experience is anything like mine, this summary will inundate you with racialized memories. We will follow the same process we did in our exploration of gender identity. I begin my interrogation with a list of racialized memories of my own.

Growing up ensconced in a predominately white area—on a farm just outside Shelby, Ohio, then a thriving community—all white, mostly Protestant (Catholics lived and went to elementary and junior high school a few miles from the town), only two Italian families—the town's photographer and shoe repairman.

Attending an all-white high school from 1956–59, with a curriculum that was all too silent on the repercussions of antiblackness.

Listening to a relative make a racist generalization about Chinese people in the presence of my daughter, who was then engaged to a Chinese-American (my daughter and I were counseled that our family, ensconced in their all-whiteness, justified this by saying that they simply weren't socially conscious of racial differences—they really weren't hateful, a belief I have come to understand as racist, thanks to Ibram X. Kendi's *How to Be an Antiracist*. Kendi argues that there are not "not racist" ideas, only racist and antiracist ones).[14]

The shock of realizing my next-door roomies as a first-year student at Baldwin-Wallace College were black, and my shameful failure to interact with them (I should add that there were only a handful of black people on the entire campus, even though it was located in the suburbs of Cleveland).

The lack of diversity in my first teaching job in Hudson, Ohio, in my master's program at Penn State, and again as a teacher in Shrewsbury, Massachusetts.

Culture shock at the age of twenty-six, when I joined my Italian husband on a Fulbright in Manila, and gratitude for the many Filipinos who were so kind to us, gratitude also for the opportunity for visits to a squatter community, Mahirap, with anthropologist Richard Stone; gratitude for a six-week stay near Sarawak on the island of Borneo.

Thirty-five years (1968–2003) among the many races and ethnicities on the islands of Hawai'i, which brought awareness of and sadness over the treatment of native Hawai'ians, who have their own Trail of Tears story of deprivation from their land.

Teaching young people from the islands at the University of Hawai'i and growing in my knowledge about racial (in)justice in the process.

Visits from my daughter's Chinese-American boyfriend, now husband of twenty-some years, getting to know his family, and appreciating his cultural traditions, especially the food.

The thrill of learning that Stacey Adams won the Democratic party nomination for governor of Georgia, the first black woman nominated for this office, contrasted with disappointment over her loss, and fury over possible vote tampering that may have contributed to it. Ten years in Atlanta taught me how prejudice pervades the politics of Georgia, as it does in much of the South.

A book club discussion of Kathryn Stockett's *The Help* during my time in Atlanta that danced around the awfulness of the long history of Southern treatment of black people—the families of several of our members had black servants growing up.

Take a deep breath and list your own racialized experiences, to get at (in)civilities. As you are not an anthropologist, this process may seem

unfamiliar, perhaps challenging and intimidating. Formidable as it may be, now it is time to list significant moments in your own racialized past. We are now at the heart of our interrogation.

The goal is to understand experiences of your racial heritage as honestly as you can, to answer, "Who am I?" So, turn to your journal, make your list, naming an item per page so you can elaborate later. Date your entries so you can associate further insights with your initial responses. You will have rich analysis to bring to your civility circle, and insights will arise in the discussion.

Unpacking White Privilege

The scholar Ibram X. Kendi would describe what I experienced among the citizens in Shelby as denial, which occurs when "the person defends his superior sense of self, his racially unequal society." Kendi believes Donald Trump is unifying Americans in this denial of racism. He explains that these denials "come from both conservatives and white liberals who think people of color are stuck in cycles of unstable families and criminal cultures, and that the deprivations of poverty and discrimination spin out bad people."[15]

As a professor who regularly taught our department's "Introduction to the Study of Language," I am drawn to Kendi's concept of a "new vocabulary" list that has been developed "to evade admissions of racism."[16] Have you, or has anyone you know, thoughtlessly used phrases such as "welfare queen" that resort to outright name-calling, along with the suggestion of undue reliance on welfare? For a different take on our interrogation, find time—in your journal or in discussion with members of your civility circle—to figure out how the following examples work to maintain white privilege and to deny social justice. As you read through the list, notice the irony in the naming. How does each of the following items from Kendi's list evoke historic and present practices of racism and what they have wrought for its victims?

law and order	colorblind	war on drugs	post-racial
model minority	illegal immigrant	Obamacare	achievement gap
handout	blue lives matter	no excuses	personal responsibility

We see that naming itself is an injustice, in that it gives a false sense of circumstances and history.

It is difficult for those of us who have lived in white privilege to see our own situations as such, and to see the racism that underpins them. Robin Diangelo's *White Fragility: Why It's So Hard for White People to Talk about Racism* opened my eyes. Her chapter headings for "How Does Race Shape the Lives of White People" are revelatory: Belonging, Freedom from the Burden of Race, Freedom of Movement, Just People, White Solidarity, The Good Old Days, White Racial Innocence, and Segregated Lives. These concepts have likely informed some people's thinking about race, and perhaps their excuses for racist behavior.

Our civility commitment challenges racialized behavior. We want societal change. We reach full humanity when we address racism in our lives and communities. When we do, we will be breathing life into a new civility.

Unpacking a Personal, Racialized Experience

Calling out our racialized experiences is revelatory, yet we need to dig deep into our psyches and look at our experiences through a civility lens to get to fairness.

Let me unpack a related term by using personal examples: culture shock.

The culture shock I experienced in Manila at age twenty-six was my first coming-to-terms with racial differences. Filipinos are of Asian, Pacific Island, and Spanish descent, many a real mixture, as so many people are in my own country. I tagged along on my husband's Fulbright, not truly engaged in his cross-cultural psychology project, more witness to it.

Intellectually, I believed that I was not racist; interpersonally, the shock of the difference and too much time on my hands led me to depression (a life-long tendency), made me hold back, and kept me from fully immersing myself in the opportunity. I had vaulted from my experience of white privilege into an unfamiliar culture.

We lived in lower-level rooms of a wealthy Filipino family—more privilege. I was treated with care and kindness everywhere I turned. Not a person failed to welcome me and to help me understand the culture. Filipinos were interested in how theirs differed from mine. I gave my best effort to cultural immersion, though, and eventually we were able to laugh over our differences.

I understand now that my immersion was gentle, different from many if not most cultural immersions. The shock was simply the difference—the unfamiliarity, the new setting, languages, food, and customs (we were to hire a maid for our few needs, as we lived in a larger home and the maids there insisted that, out of fairness to them, we must have one too). My ability to recover came, I think, from a point of view that embraced difference, although until that year I had little idea of what difference really meant.

My experience makes a good case for the anthropological argument that race is about social and cultural differences. The meanings I came to were ones that my Filipino friends and I ascribed to them. The range of skin color was immense, from the darker complexion of our maid Vangie to the light skin of Imelda, and the in-between skin tones of the Barons, the dear family with whom we lived, whose three little boys used to peek in our bedroom window.

I learned much of full humanity that year and came away with an authentic understanding of what making common cause really means. I cringe when I read of human rights abuses that Rodrigo Duterte is now carrying out.

Now it is your turn. Interrogate your racial heritage, using my example above along with the three-question set as a guide. Assuming you live in the United States, you will be describing your role in its racial heritage for the years you have lived and the places you have lived, noting if you have resisted or participated in discriminatory behavior. It takes courage to speak out.

Journaling Prompts: Race

Full Humanity—Interdependence of Us All—Common Ground for Common Cause

- *Who am I as [insert race name]?* How has this influenced my core being?

- *How have I othered?* How have I treated those of different race(s) with prejudice or without acknowledging them or including them in my world? In what ways did I engage in racialized denial?

- *How have I been othered, treated as an other, with prejudice, with neglect?* Mention a few examples of when and how racial barriers have been removed, with genuine caring interactions.

  - ° How have I brought fairness and generosity to racialized situations? How have I suppressed, maybe eventually eliminated, my own prejudices and discrimination, moving myself to inclusivity and therefore civility? How have I helped others to do so?

- *How might I move my insights on race to actions on behalf of civility?* How have I already done so?

Interrogating Identity: Religion—Toward Fairness

Religion is almost impossible to define. A dictionary will probably define [religion] easily: a system that believes in a higher power, has an organization, provides moral rules, uses books that are said to be authoritative, and so on. These characteristics are useful to think about, and are often found, but there are also exceptions. For me, a religion is a complex of people, words, music, art, and ritual that together lead individuals to experience wonder and mystery.
—Michael Molloy

Let us center our discussion with a few observations:
- There are hundreds of religions across the world, but a few predominate: Christianity, Islam, Hinduism, Buddhism, or no religious affiliation;
- Religions have been major carriers of moral and ethical principles, faith, and values;
- The world's religions have a history of dissension within them, and prolonged and devastating wars between and among them;

- Many of the world's population commit deeply to creeds and dicta of their religions' sacred gods and texts, and see their own religion as sacrosanct;

- Compared to other countries in the world, American society has relatively few who practice non-Christian traditions;

- Settlers came to America seeking religious tolerance;

- The American Constitution supports separation of church and state;

- A strong evangelistic strain exists in American Protestant religious tradition, and representatives of this group played a major role in the 2016 election and continue to be an influential force;

- There is a vibrant black Protestant tradition in America;

- Some two percent of Americans commit to Mormonism, with Utah and Idaho having the largest populations;

- Over one-fifth of Americans declare themselves unaffiliated, although some of them still profess a belief in God or spirituality, while some commit to atheism and agnosticism.

Religion is a major force in our lives (whether or not one is necessarily religious), in our society, and in our history.

Much of the world's conflict is mired in ethnocentric religious beliefs, often tied to place, ethnicity, and politics. Hundreds die daily across our global village in wars that have some basis in religious beliefs. Think of Arab-Israeli and Shia-Sunni conflicts, the war in Afghanistan, the Global War on Terrorism that has its basis in ISIS, and so on. In America at present there is vigorous political debate over our participation in these ongoing wars.

Religious discrimination is at issue in the Trump presidency, through his favoritism of the religious right—particularly white Evangelicals—and through his travel ban, which some believe is an attempt to ban Muslims.

Votes are being cast over religious beliefs that go to our faith and spiritual convictions, our reason for being, and concern for our afterlife. The subject seems almost beyond reach. But our quest here is to bring civility home, to see how it plays itself out in our lives.

What Role Has Religion Played in Your Life?

Let us reflect on the interplay of religion and civility in our community and country. We do so with the insights of our identity interrogations so far. Themes from our interrogation of gender identity and of race inform our consideration.

Our controlling question goes to how we channel our personal religious energy in the service of civility and encourage those religions with which we are affiliated to do the same. Churches are concerned with our conversion and salvation, but they also do their religious work in a social/cultural/political setting. Here in the United States, they enjoy a tax-exempt status that enriches their coffers. In exchange, the social contributions they make are immense, through various community programs, such as feeding the poor and eldercare. At issue, though, is how much they exploit their tax exemptions to promote faith-based policies and politics.

For many, religion deals with one's personal relationship with a higher power, hope for an afterlife, and rules for abiding in our world. It offers the comfort of ritual, with its prayers, music, and concern for one's soul. Everyone, even those of you who identify with no religion, can be vigilant, insisting through your actions and vote that churches do their share to advance civility as we understand it.

Burning issues, though, come to the fore: the Catholic Church's cover-up of pedophilia and sexual abuse and its subsequent failure to take action; the secondary, or complementarian, role that women are assigned in so many religions, based on a literal reading of the Bible that is not in synchrony with civil laws; its rejection of the LGBTQ+ community that is not in keeping with recent Supreme Court rulings; a creationist view that rejects the scientific understanding of evolution and the workings of the universe, and that indeed inhibits the advance of science and the contributions that scientists can make in saving our planet. These issues go to religion's stake in our public life.

So now we turn to how religion has marked our personal lives. We can interrogate by storytelling. Notice how my stories below unpack my religious identity. You can write stories too, now that you have internalized the interrogative process. Read mine by way of comparison, then write your own.

The Methodist church was a dominant force in the first eighteen years of my life. My family attended church weekly—sometimes there or at one led by my maternal Uncle Walter in the Evangelical United Brethren Church, with its riveting sermon and gospel hymns, Uncle Walter's voice emotional and resonant in contrast to Reverend Scott's meek style. After fifty years of thinking of the Bible as a great work of literature rather than the word of God, I have difficulty recalling anything other than its basic tenets, stories, poems, and prayers.

I love religious music, which to this day resonates in my soul. I played piano fairly well (organ minimally), so I know classic religious music and hymns. I accompanied the men's Sunday School class as they sang beloved hymns to open their study. Just this year I was prompted to join the Universalist-Unitarian Church, and I am still in awe of what music can bring to peace of mind: a reverent place, mindful quiet, extending myself into the music, its vibrations entering my soul. From music, I have come to appreciate solitude and so easily slide into mindful awareness.

Religious commitment suffused my home life, thanks to Mother's reminders to live with love and to be kind and caring, beginning with us. Mother's faith seemed unwavering, although her life presented challenges that would have caused many a good Christian to fail. My father's faith, if he had it, was unstated. He saw that we got to church and were well dressed and comported, and was unwavering in his support of Mother's insistence on and demonstration of caring.

A half-dozen Protestant churches thrived in our little town (fewer today), and I sensed righteous competition among them. Looking at my maternal and paternal family over my lifetime, I testify that religion can turn righteous people to self-righteousness. A discussion about Catholics could evoke a self-satisfied, holier-than-thou attitude from my well-meaning, Methodist family members. We thought we attended the "best" of the Christian churches. Methodists were better than Lutherans or Presbyterians because of doctrinal differences that were never explained, and I never understood.

As my belief in God changed, I held on to a caring, "do unto others" philosophy. I carried that as I encountered new cultures with their unfamiliar religions in the Philippines and Borneo, and later in my life as a professor teaching in cross-cultural Hawai'i. I lived comfortably with the difference of others; I appreciated it, and, at times, treasured it.

There are bruises from my religious decisions: three siblings fear for my soul in the afterlife, no matter my goodness in the here and now; two seem tolerant; and the one who has predeceased us would have voted with the majority. Their sadness over my beliefs indicates how critical religion is, not only in my family but in so many of our lives.

My narrative ends up being a commitment to doing good, day by day in the here and now, a belief central to civility, with its commitment to place and principle. My faith in humankind is strong. I believe that when I die the energy of my life force will translate into the life force of my surroundings, people, and place.

Now is your chance to summarize stories that shape your religious identity—with an eye to how the positive biases of loving care stand against the negative ones of prejudice. How has religion, or lack of religion, taught you to live ethically, to bring love and caring to your communities, to look at your world with a broader perspective of concern and action? How have you developed a moral code to guide life's choices? Has religion or spirituality played a role in the development of your moral code? If so, how?

Religion and Civility: A Personal Choice that Aligns with Civility

We must hold on to intelligence, reason, and science to pursue truth, in whatever arena. So I turned to humanism. The words of William R. Murry, from *Reason and Reverence: Religious Humanism for the 21st Century*, speak for me:

> I am a humanist because I believe in the inherent worth and dignity of every person, because I believe life is most worth living when we strive to make the world a better place, and because I believe the only possibility for a world in which love, justice, peace, and freedom prevail is through human beings working together to transform the world.[17]

He continues:

> To be religious is a matter of one's attitude toward all of life. The religious
> aspect of humanism consists of . . . reverence and wonder at the world
> of nature, at human creativity, and at life itself; a sense of the unity of
> all things; joy in human community; and a commitment to a cause that
> transcends the self.[18]

Like William Murry, "More than a belief in a deity, I believe these values define what it means to be religious."[19] I find the Unitarian Universalist Church of Akron is true to the commitments described above. Its members constitute a civility community of activists for social and racial justice. I have learned from classes on poetry, humanism, spirituality, white privilege, and antiblackness. I am a member of both its fiction and nonfiction book clubs. I applaud the initiatives of UU (Unitarian Universalists), Black Lives Matter, and SURJ (Showing Up for Racial Justice).

I also appreciate the reverence and ritual of Sunday church: the organ, choir, and singing of hymns, candle-lighting, readings, sermons—all of which inspire the joy and wonder Mike Molloy speaks of in this section's epigraph. Our Commitment to Service is said in both English and Spanish; our children are cherished; the LGBTQ+ community is welcome and in attendance. Sunday services devoted entirely to music (twice a year) are divine. Our band turns up now and then to add musical variety. Some in our church believe in God and life hereafter. Others do not. We coexist.

Now it's your turn. Open your journal. In our quest for civility, we ask: how do our religious belief systems, to the extent we have them, square with civility? We are on sacred ground here. But should not the sacred be able to meet the civil and engage in dialogue over the guiding principles of each?

We are answering the "Who am I?" question, interrogating biases and prejudices—and loving and caring—that grow from religious beliefs; answering "Who am I?" as a religious being. We are also weaving our gendered, racial, and religious identities together—to see how they reinforce one another to contribute to the totality of who we are—and to see how that totality is consonant with our civility commitment.

Journaling Prompts: Who Am I as a Function of My Religious Beliefs?

Full Humanity—Interdependence of Us All—Common Grounds for Common Cause

- *Who am I as [insert religious beliefs]?* How have religious beliefs and traditions shaped who I am?

- *How have I othered?* How have I treated those who hold religious beliefs different from my own?

- *How have I been othered because of my religious beliefs?*

- *How might I move these insights on religious beliefs to actions on behalf of civility?* How have I already done so?

  ○ How have I risen above prejudicial behavior and acted with equanimity in religious discussions and disputes? How have I been treated with decency in the face of religious differences?

  ○ In what public ways can I bring the principles of civility to the challenges that religious prejudices present in our society: To immigration policy? To tolerance advocacy? To interfaith discussions? To church-community cooperatives for social causes? To urge my church toward public activism, toward peace, for example, or any number of social or civic causes?

  ○ In what ways might I help the people and practices of my own church rise to the challenges of civility? To deal with racial and sexual discrimination? To deal with historical and actual injustices to members of its congregations? To be more inclusive? To address social justice issues of the day?

Interrogating: Politics—Toward Fairness

The United States Constitution, together with our Bill of Rights and its subsequent amendments, create a context in which political civility can flourish.

Indeed, one of the goals of our introspection is to understand democracy, with its power of civility, as a central force in the world. As usual, we are concerned with the global force and fate of civility, so we look at the promise of an integrated world democracy driven by the tenets of civility.

To that end, I'm drawn to Charles Krauthammer's idea of "democratic realism," which Marc A. Thiessen cites in his tribute to Krauthammer. He writes,

> Charles [supports] what he called democratic realism, which "sees as the engine of history not the will to power, but the will to freedom." America, he [says], "will support democracy everywhere, but we will commit blood and treasure only in places where there is a strategic necessity." Put another way, he [says], we will intervene "where it counts." Germany and Japan counted. So did the Soviet Union. So does the battle against Islamic totalitarianism.[20]

We have witnessed the will to power in other countries where democratic institutions have been subverted, as in Georgia, Hungary, Nicaragua, Peru, the Philippines, Poland, Russia, Sri Lanka, Turkey, and Ukraine.[21]

How can we oppose "the will to power" and sustain "the will to freedom"? One powerful way is through the practice of civility: the "will to freedom" of "democratic realism" goes hand in hand with the principles of civility.

Harvard professors of government Steven Levitsky and Daniel Ziblatt, co-authors of *How Democracies Die*, define the principled behavior we might hope for in our congressional leaders. The principles apply to lower legislative bodies as well, in our states, counties, cities, and towns. They apply to the reasoning we as citizens bring to our political decisions, even as politics influences and informs our identity markers of gender, race, and religion.

Levitsky and Ziblatt first explain how democracy has been subverted by leaders worldwide who possess four indicators of authoritarian behavior:

- Rejection of (or weak commitment to) democratic rules of the game;
- Denial of the legitimacy of political opponents;
- Toleration or encouragement of violence; and
- Readiness to curtail civil liberties of opponents, including media.[22]

They write,

> In extraordinary times, courageous party leadership means putting
> democracy and country before party and articulating to voters what is
> at stake. When a party or politician . . . emerges as a serious threat [to
> democratic principles], there is little alternative. United democratic
> fronts can prevent extremists from winning power, which can mean sav-
> ing a democracy.[23]

Inherent in our effort after civility is not only a call for a united democratic front but also for our political parties to assume leadership. Levitsky and Ziblatt remind us that "[t]he real protection against would-be
authoritarians. . . .[are] the gatekeepers—our political parties."[24]

Levitsky and Ziblatt mourn "the great Republican abdication" our
citizens are witnessing—Republican legislators giving over too much
authority to a leader who threatens democracy. We regret too the political
polarization of both parties that results in legislative impasses. With Levitsky and Ziblatt, those of us seeking a new civility in Congress ask that
two practices guide political party behavior—(1) mutual toleration, or
patient self-control, and (2) institutional forbearance, or restraint and
tolerance.[25] It is worth noting that patient self-control, restraint, and tolerance inform our identity exploration.

Those of us who seek a new civility yearn for a president and a Congress who play by the rules and who resist a retreat into a tribalism or partisanship that constrains a democratic spirit and drives both to impasse.

For civility to flourish, all of us must have the courage of our convictions, legislators first and foremost. Too often our legislators have been
last and least in holding to their principles. We ask them to wield their
power in the name of civility.

The stories of Gandhi in India, Nelson Mandela in South Africa, and
Martin Luther King in the United States offer profiles of the political
courage it takes for exceptionality. Their quests in the name of nonvio-
lence helped create a civil climate on a national and international level.
Now each of us can do the same on a personal level. Indeed, we are chan-
neling Gandhi, Mandela, and King on our civility journey. Can we not
ask the same of our elected officials?

Politics and Control: Power Dynamics at the Personal Level

Politics can be thought of as the total complex of relations between people, or as conduct in a particular area of experience, as in family politics, or office politics, and ethnic politics. Politics can also be thought of as "the art or science concerned with winning and holding control"[26]—usually over a government. As our interrogations begin personally, it is appropriate to think about the politics of our personal lives. It is a touchy subject, yet our interrogations begin in the realm of the personal, in our homes and communities. Society seems to be growing more comfortable with the personal: it is out there in our society, through the introduction of cell phones and the screen time that messaging, Facebook, and Twitter have brought with them.

So where to begin? A key word is control. Ask yourself how the issue of fairness was managed in your family: who held/holds control—when, where, how, and why? I describe my experience below. Read it, comparing your experience of the politics of control.

> The dynamics of control in my life are a function of my age and of my gender, born at the tail end of the Silent Generation, when women's work was in the home and relationship roles were traditionally defined.
>
> My father held the reins in our family of nine. My mother overtly complied with his direction. Husband in driver's seat, in control; wife in compliance, and at the same time analyzing the situation as a teaching experience for her children. She guided us morally, practically, and to some extent politically, the assumption being that we would be educated and in charge of our own decision-making, reminding us to learn from our circumstances, with attention to the burdens of her life in particular. Weekly trips to the library in town, which she squeezed into our schedule no matter what, shaped us into readers, which gave us an avenue to informed decision-making, including voting.
>
> Mother taught me how listening can be an act of power: as the first step in changing minds, as in when mother listened to father's objections about sending us to college. Her patient listening ultimately convinced him that twin Judy and I should go to college.
>
> Listening taught me to attain deep focus amidst the confusion of many bodies, several chores, competing needs. There was no excuse for not

listening well. My twin and I were observers, listeners, and questioners, Judy leading the way, with me playing backup and acting as a smoother of ruffled feathers.

Of physical and emotional abuse, there was some—it was an acceptable form of discipline at the time. I received one spanking because of misbehavior at a Grange Hall meeting at which my twin and I had sung songs to mother's accompaniment. All three of my brothers received whippings with belts—these occurred out of mother's sight; watching her sons being whipped was pure torture to her, as she thought whipping to be unnecessary.

Product of my times, I married a man with as much force of energy as my father and lived fifty years in a marriage, accommodating his personality and needs. I learned from him to appreciate and understand the complexities of culture(s), and the power dynamics they held. Through him, the liberal thinking that mother inspired grew to full-blown liberalism and a life as a secular humanist. With him, I absorbed the beauty of the Hawai'ian Islands, mourned the power dynamics that robbed Hawai'ians of so much of their land and culture, and learned from the many students from diverse cultures that populate the University of Hawai'i.

With our administrative positions, we lived with and through power dynamics at home and at work (promotion and tenure applications, the competition of departments and campuses within the university, the university's position within the state). Power plays all around.

We tried to make the marriage work until, in retirement, I finally understood I was losing myself, no longer having a career into which I could pour my mind and energy and caring. I divorced him—in this case, an ultimate act of personal power.

In healthy relationships, the dynamics of control are understood and people in them agree to play by rules. How have the dynamics of control played themselves out in your life? How did you cope? Did you resist? Did you learn self-control? To what end? Did the dynamics of control ever turn to power struggles? To what end? Or did your home offer a model of good behavior? Of civility? If so, how so?

Linking Personal Experience to Politics, Local and National

Our exploration of power in our personal lives prepares us to understand something of the dynamics of power—and the control, authority, and influence that comes along with it—in the practice of politics on the public stage. We assume the dynamics are even more complex when the life of a town, city, county, state, or country is at stake. Just as in personal life, beliefs and the behaviors have consequences.

Yet it is not enough for us to create civility only in our personal lives. Our public lives and the public institutions by which we govern ourselves must also create a new civility through their beliefs and behaviors. So, we must broaden our scope, keeping in mind how our politics intersect with gender, race, and religion.

In concluding our thoughts about politics as power, and in connecting the personal to the political, let us consider the Equal Rights Amendment that will provide constitutionally for the legal equality of the sexes and prohibit discrimination on the basis of sex. It was passed by the US Senate in 1972 and referred to the states for ratification. It had been introduced in 1923, soon after 1920 when, after nearly a century of effort, women were given the right to vote, known as suffrage. As of January 2019, it was one state away from ratification. Recent efforts for ratification have failed in Virginia, Arizona, and Florida. Other states that have not ratified are Alabama, Arkansas, Georgia, Louisiana, Mississippi, Missouri, North Carolina, Oklahoma, South Carolina, and Utah. I mention the ERA because it is another attempt after justice, an attempt that is at the feet of politicians in the states mentioned above. This challenge allows us a segue to the public and the political, to those politicians who serve us at the local, state, and national levels.

What kind of people do we want in control? How reasonably will they allocate precious resources and tax dollars? How will they address our concerns for social and racial justice? Given our democratic framework, people in office have the potential to help citizens to their full humanity. The process of electing representatives demonstrates our interdependence; we are at the mercy of the victors' judgments.

How have political issues on the national scene impacted your personal life, as they so surely did in the lives of women who advocated for equal rights in the early part of the last century?

What must we do, as citizens, in our full humanity, claiming the ideal, hoping for a way to address common cause?

First and foremost, commit to the idea that one person can make a difference.

Respect the power of the vote, the privilege to vote.

Vote. Rally others to the voting booth. Imagine every person exercising that power. Imagine no one who is eligible to vote being kept from doing so.

Educate yourself on voter issues. Imagine every person mobilizing energy and sharing information about the issues of the day.

Contribute to local public interest groups. This is where citizens can make a huge difference. Imagine bolstering interest in voting and getting voters to the polls.

Take an active role in the party that most aligns with your carefully considered political views. Imagine attending party meetings and voicing your concerns. Do the hard work of campaigning for a candidate in whom you believe. Run for office yourself.

This is the work of citizen. This is how we bring the tenets of civility to politics.

Study the processes at work in the elections of both parties, trying to understand strategies, the use of campaign funds and of social media networks. Listen for accountability. Think not only of the vote you intend to cast but also of how election processes and campaign rhetoric are affecting our country.

Resist the tribalism of identity politics, the temptation to attach to your own race, religion, or immigration philosophies as a sole reason for identifying with a candidate or party. With identity politics comes extreme partisanship and often anger toward and disdain for opposition candidates.

Do not hunker down with a lack of caring for other people(s). Do not engage in name-calling, shaming, outright lying, or vulgarization. Examine your prejudices. Look to bring unconscious bias into consciousness, and act on the revelations.

During and after elections, look for balanced sources of information. Don't just stay tuned to one source of political news. (Exploration #5 on Reasoning Well has some rudiments for asking good questions about political situations and motives, and for providing good information yourself.) Deconstruct fake news. Think carefully of the value of social media as a way of influencing judgments, and as a mechanism for free publicity.

So, how well have I done in living up to my own imperatives?

I have voted in every major election.

My study of rhetorical traditions, which I bring to the fore in Process #5 on Reasoning Well, provided me with a good basis for analysis of political rhetoric.

My experience and concern for civility bring a global, long-term scope to my political vision. Its liberal tendencies were enhanced by three-plus decades in liberal academia and blue Hawai'i.

I worry over the lack of civility in campaign conduct, so apparent in negative advertising. Can the power of our democratic institutions override the incivilities of a particular person, when that person is a world leader? Does the framework of our democracy as it is defined and practiced have the civility-sustaining, moderative effect that I hope for? Do politicians have the wherewithal to cast their vote for civility? Ultimately, to do so, they will have to give up extreme partisanship. Will our country, and hence democracy itself, have a diminished presence in the world as a function of one president's incivilities? Time will tell. There is comfort in knowing our democracy has survived, notwithstanding a series of leaders with shortcomings of different sorts. Some answers to these questions will have played out by the time you read this book. Another set will have arisen.

My concern for an enduring civility is prompted by grave concern about power politics of the international scene: dangerous, continually evolving wars in the Middle East and the United States' involvement in continually evolving wars; Putin and Russia's threat, as felt in Eastern Europe, the Middle East, and here in the United States; Duterte in the Philippines; Kim Jong Un in Korea; the uncertainties in our relationship with China;

the refugee situation in Europe, Africa, the Middle East, and here in the United States. Regime changes on several continents. Big issues for a state department with reduced ranks, and a leader who communicates through 280-character tweets.

On review, I'm a better citizen now than when I was young. I can remember my undergraduate English 100 Professor, Neil Shoemaker, and his shock that none of us were reading the newspaper regularly, and that all of us were so ill-informed on contemporary events. I felt the same chagrin over my own English 100 students' behavior.

I appreciate facts. I appreciate the need to be well informed. I'm appalled that many citizens cannot name the three branches of government or describe how they function to balance power. I'm dismayed that so few people vote.

I'm less self-centered, more community-centered, than when I was young. I have gained wisdom with age, time, and reflection. I appreciate strength of character while recognizing the fragilities of life. And so, I search for civility.

Having read my narrative of the evolution of my political identity, turn to journaling again, make some notes, craft your own political identity narrative, read it to members of your civility circle, and examine how pairing civility with politics—indeed, with any one of our four markers, helps us find our way to common cause.

Linking Politics and Civility

Let me begin this final section on interrogating our politics with a plea to all elected legislators: please join our civility crusade. Do not abdicate the role you were elected to carry out. Your inaction on critical issues denies the very role you voluntarily undertook. Your inaction weakens the structure, the very pillars, of democracy. Your inaction is an ultimate act of incivility, not only to the structure of democracy but also to the faith of the citizenry.

Legislators, how will you address party partisanship? Will you put aside party dogma and loyalty and make necessary compromises to pass decent legislation on immigration and health care, for example? Will you

insist that other legislators put democracy and country before party affili-
ations? Will you recognize political parties as gatekeepers of democracy?
Will you create a healthy bipartisanship in Congress?

Let me follow up with a plea to citizens: educate yourselves on the
issues facing your elected politicians. Where will you pitch in to enact
civility and to sustain the strength of our democracy?

Legislators and citizens, how will you provide a counterforce to our
erratic president, whose behaviors result in a troubling uncertainty over
critical events on the world stage and here at home? What will you do about
the pressing problems listed below?

Racial and gender injustices loom large, intersecting in one way or
another with politics, place, class, and opportunities for education.

Our middle class shrinks, with wealth going to a miniscule few, while
poverty ravages our lower class.

Gun violence and school shootings continue, as our Congress is held
hostage by the dollars and influence of the NRA. A gun epidemic rages
across our country.

Simultaneously, America's international role is tenuous, as the possibility of nuclear warfare is in the hands of a leader known to rush to ill-
informed judgment, known not to read his one-page summaries of significant events—as he leads a democracy that depends on reasoning and
literacy, on being well-informed in a number of arenas, not just those of
Fox News or popular tweets.

Large corporations drive the world economy as much as nation-states
themselves, a tendency that will certainly impact our democratic institutions, a tendency that is dollar-driven more certainly than it is humanely
driven.

America's international political role is shifting with China and
Russia, with their strongmen leadership of Xi Jinping and Putin, a continuing threat.

Wars in the Middle East, Southeast Asia, and South Asia rage on. Our
veterans come home to suffer neglect.

Those of us committed to creating civility define ourselves as activists.
Affirming the dictum that "all politics is local," we go to work in our
neighborhoods and communities. Each of us wields power, perhaps more
than we realize—both through the dynamics of control in our home and

family, and in the public power dynamics of our communities.[27] May this new understanding of political identity be manifested carefully yet powerfully in the communities we call home.

Identity and the Quest for Fairness

You have just completed an intensely profound, personal, sometimes intimate, critical interrogation that examined your history, beliefs, practices, errors in judgment, causes for rejoicing, discord, harmony, and promises.

You completed identity interrogations on gender, race, politics, and religion. These subjects are central to living and understanding your life, taking into account what is happening on the personal and public, local and national scene. Our interrogation pulled no punches. It asked hard questions. The answering took you through challenging terrain—some rougher than others, given the amount of forethought, attitude, and biases you brought to the interrogation. I'm certain there was resistance, the questions pushing hot buttons for one reason or another.

You have read your life as text. These four interrogations above took you indirectly into the territory of age, mind/body ability as defined in DNA, places lived, social class and the earning power it allows, education, ethnicity and its issues of social and religious customs, food, and dress that sit so closely alongside race. We acknowledge those markers as central to your identity. You are familiar enough by now with the set of interrogative questions that you can consider how they intersect with the markers you have already discussed.

You dealt with my opinions and identity, different from yours in so many ways. Doing so gives you practice in dealing with difference.

All in all, the questions were tough going, but I hope you found relief in your lists and memories that allowed you to tell your identity story. Personal reflection can be powerful in so many ways.

Think of the interrogation itself as a cleansing—getting those biases out in front of you so you can deal with them so that you can address the negativity that may be pulling you down and may be punishing to others. Not that I don't realize you have a gazillion other demands on your daily life—taking care of your family, earning a living, dealing with health issues, and so on. Still, the results of the inquiry, if they yield insight, can weave their way into your very being, and those that surround you.

No denying it, in taking on the mantle of citizen, we need the courage of warriors, the insights of great philosophers, and the compassion of great thinkers to sustain us. Once we embody even a smidgen of their qualities, we gain what we might call civility resilience, so we can manifest it in our bodies (more of that in Process #2), and send out resilience wherever we travel in our wondrous life (more of that in Process #3) and to whomever we meet (more of that in Process #4), in a responsible way (more of that in Process #5).

The past is over. What we have is now. Our future holds possibility, but no certainty. Being fully human, we live in community; those of us in that community, whatever the size, are interdependent; and that interdependence makes it desirable for us to find common ground for public good—in the name of a free, democratic life.[28]

So, write and reflect, and then bring your identity understanding to the life you are living. Then reflect on what happens. And so, insight expands, and civility is nourished.

Intersectionality Among Ten Markers of Identity: A Synopsis

Those we are born with	*Those first defined in home*	*Those shaped in our lives*
DNA-defined self	class	religion
age/year of birth/time	ethnicity	politics
sex	place	education
race		

We have just looked at how identity shapes our civil behavior, looking at the markers of gender, race, religion, and politics, and only beginning to think about how they impinge on one another. But we oversimplify if we do not look at the complexity of interactions among all markers. So, although we only looked at four in our analysis above, I lay ten of them out here, so that you can analyze how they interact and impact you as you go through your days.

There is potentiality in each of the markers; you can change, at least to some extent, what has been "assigned" to you at birth. There is the possibility for change in all ten markers, really, except the time you are born, which is firm. You are far enough along in your life that you can see the change that has occurred within each marker-category since your birth. Further, you can project what you see for yourself within each of the markers for the time you have left on this good earth. And further yet, you can imagine how the civility paradigm we are constructing will play out in your life and how you might work to change the incivilities within each of the markers. The purpose of our civility journey, after all, is to allow all of us to flourish.

The interactions are exponential.

In your civility journal, work through the inflections that are most critical to your life. The questions will read something like this (starting with two of the biggies):

How has your identity been inflected or altered by the circumstances of your race? Your class? Your religion? Your opportunities for education? and so on.

How has your experience of race been influenced by class (a hugely critical question—class so critical to opportunity to thrive)? By education? By politics?

Journaling Prompts: Politics

Full Humanity—Interdependence of Us All—Common Ground for Common Cause

- *Who am I as a [insert political beliefs], as a politically inclined person, as a family member exercising power, and as a citizen participant in politics?*

  - *When and how have I approached political discussions with equanimity, with fairness and generosity of heart? Have I treated others with decency in face of significant political differences?*

  - *Have I looked carefully at how I align myself politically? Have I overlooked significant issues in the name of voting the ticket, or sticking with usual political choices?*

- *How have I othered? How have I treated those whose political beliefs are different from mine with prejudice or without acknowledging or including them in my world?*

- ° Have I fallen victim to the partisanship of tribal thinking, of staying with and protecting those like me, of ignoring difference? Have I fallen victim to polarization driven by racial and religious realignments or resentments?

- ° How have I been treated as an other?

- *How might I move my political insights to actions on behalf of civility? How have I already done so?*

  - ° In voting, have I thought about America's responsibility to the rest of the world, about "the will to freedom" of Krauthammer's "democratic realism," or about the sustenance of our very planet?

Process #2
Practicing Mindfulness—
Toward Awareness

Mindfulness in its creative and contemplative forms enables us individually to create more vital and open states of mind, ways of being, ways of living. Mindfulness collectively can help us sense the ways in which we are profoundly interconnected to one another, and to our home, this place we call Earth. . . .
—Daniel J. and Madeleine W. Siegel

I learned about mindfulness about the same time I began research for *Creating a New Civility*. As I began to practice mindful meditation, I understood that I was achieving within myself the very state I was writing about—an awareness that helped me to full humanity.

Mindfulness is a way of paying attention, of focusing first and foremost on oneself. The practice of mindfulness is about noticing, about interior study. Through mindfulness meditation, I felt myself as fully humane, able to be present, in each moment of now.

If an identity interrogation helped me to the full humanity of civility, why not explore how mindfulness might do so? After all, my impulses to civility and incivility are instantaneous bodily responses first and foremost, driven by some combination of fight or flight, heart-felt, soul-driven instinct or emotion.

Further, my commitment to humanity would not be full unless it were embodied. The concepts would float away unless they were of me and in me. In other words, part of the meaning of *full* in our conceptualization of full humanity is that it is of our entirety—body and heart as well as mind and soul. My search for civility, then, would need to address myself as a corporeal being. How might my very presence be an expression of civility?

The practice of mindfulness offered a possibility.

Defining Mindfulness

Mindfulness, a technique derived from Eastern meditation practices, was first described by Jon Kabat-Zinn in 1979 at the University of Massachusetts Medical School, when he led a small number of patients through a program he called mindfulness-based stress reduction (MBSR). His approach combines meditation, a bit of yoga, and a gentle yet intense mix of embodied awareness, always focused in the present moment.

Kabat-Zinn is a leading expert on mindfulness. In 1990, *Full Catastrophe Living: Using the Wisdom of Your Body and Mind to Face Stress, Pain, and Illness*, was first published. The "full catastrophe" metaphor comes from Zorba the Greek when he describes life as "the full catastrophe"—by which he means the "supreme appreciation for the richness of life and the inevitability of all its dilemmas, sorrows, tragedies, and ironies."[1] This metaphor captures so perfectly why mindfulness is essential to civility. We as citizens need a way to approach life's richness as well as the inevitability of its dilemmas, sorrows, tragedies, and ironies. In embodying mindfulness, we have a way to deal with all of them.

Kabat-Zinn has trained several generations of scholars, researchers, mental health professionals, and thousands of citizens who attended programs at his Stress Reduction Clinic at the University of Massachusetts Medical School. His conceptualization of mindfulness defines a way of being that is critical to living a life imbued in civility. It offers us as civility advocates the following:

> . . . a sense that there is a way of being, a way of looking at problems, a way of coming to terms with the full catastrophe that can make life more joyful and rich than it otherwise might be, and a sense also of being somehow more in control.[2]

Mindfulness practice can help us to that end. Process #2 introduces you to it.

Kabat-Zinn has collaborated with others in shaping the practice of mindfulness.[3] His most recent publication, *Meditation Is Not What You Think: Mindfulness and Why It Is So Important*, furthers his discussion. The magazine *Mindful* works with a definition for the popular audience that is true to Kabat-Zinn's conceptualization:

> Mindfulness is the basic human ability to be fully present, aware of where we are and what we're doing, and not overly reactive or overwhelmed by what's going on around us. Mindfulness also refers to the cultivation of this basic human ability through methods, including meditation, mind-ful movement, mindful eating, and others. We call this "mindfulness practice" to distinguish it from the basic ability.[4]

Familiarity with mindfulness will help guard against incivilities that have their home in our being. When in a contentious moment, and anger overwhelms, we can turn our mindfulness practice, take a deep breath, and abate the urge to be incivil, whether an infraction or egregiousness. We can lessen our high emotions by breathing into them. Meditative breathing is a handy meditative tool to ameliorate anger, pain, and even hate. We can lesson tension and its accompanying negative emotions through the body scan. These tools help you stay with a civil response in contentious situations.

New Understandings of the Mind

Our goal in this process is to achieve awareness. Let us turn to another of my favorite scholars, Daniel J. Siegel, for still another way of looking at mindfulness:

> The state of mindful awareness is about monitoring . . . whatever is arising as it arises. That's the receptive awareness that we are calling presence. This is the clarity that reflection builds, as it enables things to arise and simply be experienced, within awareness. . . .[5]

We aim for the clarity of awareness in Process #2. Sounds fairly simple, but the complexities or our body and mind make presence hard to achieve.

New research reveals the amazing capacity of the mind, a capacity that makes it so attuned to the practice of mindfulness, and, as we are arguing by extension, to the practice of civility. This new understanding of the mind is examined in Seigel's *Mind: A Journey to the Heart of Being Human* and, most recently, *Aware: The Science and Practice of Presence*. Drawing on his own research as a neuropsychiatrist, as well as recent research from related fields, Siegel gives a complex yet compelling explanation of the mind as a "self-organizing, emergent property of energy and information flow happening within you and between you, in your body and in your connections with others and the world in which you live."[6]

We will deconstruct that definition, and as we do so we realize that the fine array of qualities available for the work of civility: the mind is simultaneously emergent + self-organized + embodied + relational. I number the qualities below. The mind, Siegel writes,

> is (1) self-organizing,
>
> is (2) always emerging (3) energy, (4) combined with information flow, both (5) within your body and (6) between you and others,
>
> (7) connecting you as embodied, that is, as you are composed by and represented within your body,
>
> (8) to others, and
>
> (9) to the world in which you live.

Realize the implications: ideas of flow, of relationships within and between us, of connections to others, to the world in which we live—all these are abilities not usually thought of as part of the brain's capacity.

Siegel elucidates: "[e]nergy and information are within and between, and so the emergent processes arising from them would be within and between as well."[7] This inner, embodied, relational process is a far more complex way of thinking about the brain than we have had in the past.

Our brain, in other words, allows us to bring civility alive, through its accommodation of relationships and the processes involved in them. Our mind is not just inside our heads; it is in the spaces between and around us (more on this in Process #3). Imagine the power this integration gives us for rationality and for empathy. We might call this a "no excuses" conceptualization of the mind; it has the ability to handle amazing things, including the complexity and challenges of living daily life with civility.

Siegel continues, and, for clarity, I number the science fields that have been helped with this new understanding:

This view of the mind as both an embodied and relational process moves us beyond perhaps overly simple, restrictive views of mind-as-brain-activity and enables

(1) anthropologists studying culture,

(2) sociologists studying groups, and

(3) even psychologist and psychiatrists. . . .[studying] family interactions and how they shape a child's development,

to all have a *mind that emerges as much in relationships as it does from physiological, embodied processes including brain activity* (emphasis mine).

Siegel concludes: "In other words, mind seen this way could be in what seems like two places at once, as inner and inter are part of one interconnected, undivided system. In reality, these are not two places, but one system of energy and its flow. This flow arises both within us and between us."[8]

The mind's emergent capacity allows for the compassionate serenity that can come from meditation. Its embodied quality allows that sense to remain wholly with us, and to be available for us when pain, anxiety, and hopelessness arise. Its emergent, relational qualities allow the emanation of resonant vibrations that extend ourselves to others.

Siegel's research has powerful implications for civility. Our mind has power to help us behave with civility. Most striking to me is that the quartet of qualities allows the mind to emerge in relationships: I have always thought of my mind as within, not as between and among what I am contemplating. It is as if our mind's emergent capacities themselves are on the verge of civility, reaching out, for relationships.

Integrating Body, Heart, Mind, and Soul

As I grew to understand meditation, I began to realize it nourished all parts of me—my body + heart + mind + soul. To show this interrelatedness, and to remind us that we humans are constituted by these four parts, I crunch these four words into one.

My use of *bodyheartmindsoul* is not simply an affectation. The word-crunch calls out the complexity of mindfulness. As we meditate, we will think of bodyheartmindsoul as a single yet complex entity, our person-hood, our *being*. When we speak of embodying civility, we intend to convey that we are constituted by our body + heart + mind + soul.

The *heart* is often thought of as the center of our being. Its constant pulsing, day in and day out, with its own intelligence, moves blood throughout our body and sustains our lives. When we take something to heart, we internalize it, and live according to it, as we are taking civility to heart. We connect the heart to emotion, as in deep love or ache. We speak of following our heart, as if its "intelligence" is guiding a decision. Our heart is critical physiologically and metaphorically; it must be included in our naming.

The concept of soul is more challenging to define. Yours may be defined in religious terms. I think of my soul as the "best" of me beyond myself; or as that extension of my body, heart, and mind that connects me to the universe, that transfers, if you will, my molecular energy beyond myself and my life to the universe. As such, I connect spiritually to the word around me. These definitions offer a humanistic view of soul.

In claiming soul as such, I recognize my spirituality. These conceptualizations are compatible with those of James Moffett, who writes:

> To be spiritual is to perceive our oneness with everybody and everything and to act on this perception. It is to be whole within oneself and with the world. Morality ensues. From this feeling of unity proceed all positive things—wholesome, hale, healthy, and holy.[9]

It is this full sense of myself that I bring to meditation, the full sense of my identity that I now understand more completely as a result of my identity exploration. I carry that identity in my being, and my mind, with its capacity to emerge in relationships, and also, for self-understanding, to merge in my being with what has come before, with all that makes me what I am. So, my identity is woven into my bodyheartmindsoul, a kind of mindful proprioception, as it were, in which I grasp the sense of my own body and all it encompasses, including my identity, in the space of my meditative moment.

The Mindfulness Model

The concept of mindfulness has come into its own in the last several decades, through juried social-science and medical research that has affirmed its value; through therapists in various health-and education-related disciplines who have integrated mindfulness therapy into their practices; and through journalism, talk shows, and various popular culture venues that have featured its benefits. Mindfulness is a hot topic as well as a serious subject for research.[10]

I studied with psychologist Jane Eckert, who adapted Jon Kabat-Zinn's approach, as described in Williams and Penman's *Mindfulness: An Eight-Week Plan for Finding Peace in a Frantic World*. I found the positive energy of our group's shared experiences to be generative, as my insights built on the group's vibrancy and spirit. Much of what follows draws on the very positive experience of that group.

As students of mindful meditation, we will focus on two processes—meditative breathing and body scans—and show how they embody civility. Both processes culminate in the integration of bodyheartmindsoul.

In summary, mindfulness, is a slow, measured, meditative practice that involves

- systematically focusing our mind's attention on our body, its parts, and functions;
- feeling our body's response to this focused attention;
- accepting the responses, possibly emotional, maybe uncomfortable, that this attention evokes;
- accepting the totality of the experience as it is, in the here and now, in the moment by moment of its evocation; and
- understanding the wholeness of the body, its marvel as a system with a mind at its center that is at once embodied and relational.

Mindfulness requires patience and disallows hurrying. At its best, mindfulness brings peaceful relaxation. Its practice offers a foundation for our other processes. Those experienced in mindfulness often feel they are in a fully human state while they meditate, and for a while afterwards. This feeling is available for recall, a strong motivation to continue the practice.

In the near forty years since Kabat-Zinn first published his work, the worth and value of mindfulness-based approaches to cognitive therapy is beginning to be verified, although research is in its infancy. As you will see, mindfulness is so much more than a superficial, woo-woo, touchy-feely passing vogue. In a world torn with strife, mindfulness is a first step in a peace-oriented way of being—a lovely, even elegant, alternative in this crazy world.

Other cultures and past times have also shown us the power of mindfulness. It is appropriate to conclude this section with a reference to the Buddha, whose contemplative manner resonates throughout mindfulness practice. If contemporary scientists affirm the inner and inter qualities of mind, the Buddha was an early thinker who first realized and embodied them. In fact, Christians will recognize that these practices work their way through the teaching of Jesus.

I conclude this section by adding another concept—felt sense—that helps explain why mindfulness "works" so well. Eugene Gendlin, a psychologist/philosopher, uses the term *felt sense* to refer to our bodily awareness of ongoing life processes—a concept he used in his focusing oriented psychotherapy.[11]

Felt sense is a kind of nonconceptual, deep experiential knowing, a nonverbal intuitive body feel. I find that the practices of mindful awareness, which put us so deeply in touch with our bodies, make our felt sense available to us. We will identify and draw on this felt sense as we work through the exercises to follow.[12]

Our journey, as always, carries its recursive quality, curving back again to initial thoughts and integrating what we have learned and how we understand ourselves, into a fresh, fuller idea.

Now that mindfulness has been integrated into my being and my lifestyle, I meditate nearly every morning, after my coffee. I begin with a review of those I dearly love in order to center and relax myself, and then I move to variants of the processes described below. Later, I remind myself to bring the deliberation of mindfulness to daily chores, especially the ones I am tempted to rush through—tidying my kitchen, folding clothes, making the bed, and, later, ones I enjoy, such as working in my garden. I take pleasure in the process, the one that surely makes the art and experience of the Japanese Tea Ceremony so profound.

If your life permits the luxury of a mindfulness class, join one, and benefit from the structure it provides and the insights you gain from individual group members, to say nothing of the power of group dynamics.[13]

As for any new commitment, we need to create space in our lives to carry it out. Learning and practicing mindfulness takes time. With that in mind, I offer the two practices we will undertake in both a long and a short form. You need to practice the long forms before the short forms will work for you. Having done so, you can adapt the practices to suit your needs.

Our goal is to embed mindfulness into the totality of our experience so that we can turn to it in moments of high emotion, crisis, or pain. Familiarize yourself with the practices by first reading through this entire section. In doing so, you will begin to understand and integrate them into your bodyheartmindsoul.

Meditative Breathing

When you contemplate the nature of Self, you are meditating. That is why meditation is the highest state. It is the return to the root of your being, the simple awareness of being aware. Once you become conscious of consciousness itself, you attain a totally different state. You are now aware of who you are. You have become an awakened being. It's really just the most natural thing in the world. Here I am. Here I always was. . . . That is the nature of Self. That is who you are.
—**Michael A. Singer**

To learn the process, find thirty uninterrupted minutes to devote yourself to mindfulness. These minutes will be more relaxing, I promise, than the more demanding identity exploration that is still on your mind.

Eventually, you will find that you can have a restorative breathing meditation in just a few minutes. The beauty of meditation is that, once you have internalized the process, you can move through it whenever you want a break from your routine, or whenever you are in crisis and need to center yourself, always adjusting the time as necessary.

While you are learning, hold the book as you read, imagine me reading aloud to you, and then move slowly through the actions. Or find a partner to read to you as you carry out the meditation.

In reading the instructions below, proceed slowly and carry them out as you read. Meander through the words, letting them touch you, as you are touched by gentleness in your life. If you feel deprived of gentleness, the time of mindfulness, of being aware of being aware, offers gentleness to your very soul. Spread the eight steps across thirty or so minutes, with some give-and-take among the times for each step, a generous three minutes for each one, and some time for reflection upon culmination. Later you can adjust the time for circumstances.

Once your civility circle is up and running, you can begin your gatherings with a short form of this meditation. Think of this process as taking baby steps in civility.

Meditative Breathing, Shaped for Civility

To set a tone for the presence that mindfulness offers, I suggest that you meditate with a slight smile on your face, a modest one, following a Mona Lisa or Buddha smile, and drawing on the benefits of smile therapy and of positivity. Smile in your mind. Smiling is an act of civility. Resist the temptation to speed-read through what seems familiar; read at a slow, measured, contemplative pace.

1. Situate yourself in a comfortable, quiet place on a chair, sitting tall with feet on the floor, hands in your lap, giving yourself the gifts of slowing down, of quiet, of stillness.

2. Imagine yourself in harmony with your surroundings, your identity integrated with bodyheartmindsoul, in full humanity. Allow yourself to be fully present in this moment, distractions aside.

Focus on what you imagine to be your inner consciousness and simply be present in it. Have you had the privilege of hearing an orchestra? Think how orchestra members focus under the director's baton the moment the symphony is about to begin. Or perhaps you have sung in a choir, or played in an orchestra or band yourself, and can remember that focusing moment. The same focus you brought to making beautiful music is helpful here. You are bringing yourself to harmony, part of developing a civility mentality.

3. Take a slow, deep breath. Follow the breath as it moves through your body, all the way down the legs to the feet and back up again. Move your dominant hand with fingers spread wide open to your diaphragm and feel it rise and fall. (This is a good way to make sure you are belly-breathing and not chest-breathing.) Focus on the rise and fall of the diaphragm. Feel the breath moving in and out of the nostrils or mouth. Continue this process for some time.

My mantra is the phrase, "I am civility." This mantra answers the question we asked in each of the identity interrogations in Process #1, "Who am I?"

4. Slowly, on the in-breath, as belly rises and chest expands, softly say, "I am," and then on the outbreath, "civility." As you breathe, affirm, "I am civility." I work through our three civility concepts: three big body breaths, "I am full humanity"; breathe—"I am interdependent with all";

and breathe, "I am common good." Or simply drop the "I am," and let "civility" suffuse your being. Find a mantra that suits you. When "peace" seems more suitable, I say it on the inbreath, so that "peace" suffuses my body. Some people prefer simply a "hmmm."

5. Continue this deep breathing. When thoughts interfere, and they will, simply let them go. As Kabat-Zinn says, gently wave them aside—how much other time we have for them and how precious is solitude. Simply be in and with your body. We are human beings, be-ing in our bodies.

I had trouble getting to this insight. How can I continue deep breathing as I think through this problem. I am one and the same as my thinking. My thoughts drive my life! I lived a long life immersed in thoughts, my mind integrating them all. How could it be I was not my thoughts?

I suspect you will have difficulty with this "we are not our thoughts" concept too, harried and hurried as so many of our lives are. Many do. Or maybe you have what is called "monkey brain," where your thoughts skitter through your mind as monkeys skitter through trees.

Kabat-Zinn recommends addressing these issues by thinking of thoughts as clouds, separate from you, watching them pass, waving them past, returning to the solitude of mindful breathing. Do this gently.

As we continue deep breathing, understand that we are not our thoughts, an important yet difficult concept, one that is a sticking point for so many who undertake meditation. We have thoughts and can be consumed by them, but they are not the us that is the entirety of our bodies, the substance of us. Our substance is bodyheartmindsoul, not thoughts. Thoughts come and go, are ephemeral, not the stuff of us. To deal with this sticking point, I can only suggest practice, which, as in any challenging endeavor, helps one become skillful.

In mindful, meditative breathing, we put worry aside. We move into awareness of being present. Eventually this ability will help us choose our thoughts, those that we wish to attend to, and those that are detrimental to our being. The minutes that pass slowly and sometimes uncomfortably will become comfortable as we become more practiced. Remember that our approach is a process, and that process itself is integrative.

6. Attend now to what happens between breaths. Right hand over diaphragm, breathe deeply for a minute, fingers spread wide, and

notice the very, very brief pause between breaths—so brief you are barely conscious of it, say one-tenth of a second. By placing your spread hand at the base of your diaphragm, you can feel this natural pause. Take several deep breaths, and then extend the pause, just a bit.

This one-tenth of a second is significant, for one-tenth to three-tenths is said to be the amount of time it takes for the brain to receive a message, process it, and act on it.[14] In a tenth of a second, we decide and then scowl, blurt, curse, thrash out, swing, hit, take aim and fire. It has been said that the world hangs on a tenth of a second.[15] Indeed, your very life may have been shaped in a tenth of a second.

In integrating this tenth of a second into your breathing, you learn to give pause. You integrate an embodied stop-and-think process through which you can, when necessary, curb your anger, bite your tongue, cease and desist. Notice this tenth-of-a-second pause in the name of civility, for in this very brief moment you can draw on your moral center to guide a positive response, a smile or a word of lovingkindness. When we say a decision "feels right," we are drawing on our felt sense.

7. Stay with the deep breathing of mindfulness as long as time allows, as often as you can, until it becomes habit, until it feels natural. Draw on it in moments of high emotion and stress to reduce the terrible overwhelmingness of anxiety.

8. Let us end our deep breathing practice with six bodyheartmindsoul breaths, the word crunch representing us is our systemic entirety.

In mindful meditation, we breathe into our bodies, hearts, and souls under our mind's (emergent + self-organized + embodied + relational) direction. Let us recognize that it is through the solace of mindful breathing, at its best, that we embrace our souls, our precious spiritual ephemerality that is in us and of us and moves in our resonance all at the same time.

9. To bring mindful breathing to a culmination and to connect it to civility, we turn to a yoga practice similar to Earth-to-Heaven, in which you stand squarely and reach as high as you absolutely can, holding heaven, and then repeat the practice on your toes, still reaching to the heavens. You can also do this practice from the comfort of your chair.

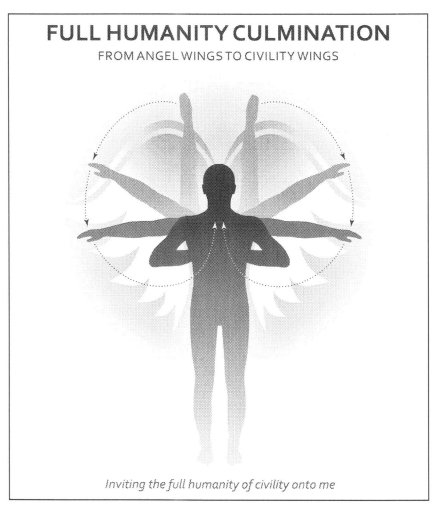

FULL HUMANITY CULMINATION

FROM ANGEL WINGS TO CIVILITY WINGS

Inviting the full humanity of civility onto me

Illustration by Susan Panning.

We name our practice civility wings. The graphic conceptualizes the practice; a glance will clarify how you mindfully send out and draw in your full humanity.

This practice draws on the angel wings that you may have made as a child after flopping down in leaves, snow, sand, or even dirt, and moving your arms and legs to make the shape of an angel's wings.

No rolling your eyes. Really do this. If you've never done yoga, you may feel uncomfortable in the practice. My grandchildren were at first, but I persisted, and eventually they saw the power of it. Now my grandson grins and sometimes greets me with civility wings. I know he has internalized the practice.

10. Feet planted firmly where you are, stretch your arms as high as you possibly can. Kabat-Zinn suggests that you reach as if you are plucking grapes from some very high vine. Repeat once or twice. Then turn to civility wings.

11. Breathing deeply and slowly, move your arms down the sides of your body, pointing fingers to your toes, and then, following your breath up your body, move your hands and arms upward next to your body, resting them momentarily over your heart, taking deep breaths as you go, the process slow and gentle. Then move your hands up, pausing them briefly at sides of your head, as if holding your integrative and relational mind inside your cranium. Then move your arms as high as you can reach. Stretch your arms up high, and then, following the pattern of angel wings, still breathing deeply and slowly, move your arms out, around, and, in a slow spiral motion on the way down, gather full humanity to you, scooping it in, and then, continuing the spiral, send out your own good vibrations of full humanity. In bringing your arms down and back into you, you are gesturing your inclusivity. Conclude civility wings by positioning your hands over your heart. You are now fully present, in presence. Let your felt sense manifest itself through angel wings transformed to civility wings.

The mindful breathing process slows us down and sets a tone for gentleness and thoughtfulness as we move through the day. Practice this relaxing process several times until you feel comfortable with it.

After you do so, you can vary it to suit your needs, adapting it to a short form, as follows. When you are in a tense moment of hurry and anxiety, take a three-minute break, sit up straight, and close your eyes. You'll want to use those three minutes to (1) breathe into your anxiety, noticing what's there— perhaps the feelings and tensions and emotions, associated with it; (2) breathe deeply and slowly, focusing on the physicality of your body as your breath moves through it, down to your toes, and then up and out through your nose or mouth; (3) and, finally, still breathing slowly and deeply, with resonance, center yourself in the here and now, ready to face what comes next.[16]

With practice, you will settle into mindful breathing comfortably. A minute or so is all you need to breathe into a tense moment, feel the emotionality, gather what is happening, and settle again into what comes next. After enough practice that you know mindful breathing from the inside out, you'll be able to use it as a tool to get you through tough times. Practice it often enough to be able to move through the steps almost instantaneously in moments of anger, anguish, difficult choices, and "I can't go on" thoughts. "Breathe into it," I tell myself, and then, very quickly, become aware, gather, and expand awareness, all in the name of settling myself down to calmness.

The Body Scan

The body scan allows you to experience the body itself even more directly than you do in meditative breathing. For the purposes of civility, we will carry it out, ever more sensitive to how the body reacts to the angst of disagreements, of trying situations, of family arguments, of deep ideological discord. Williams and Penman call it "side-stepping the ruminative mind."[17]

In writing the body scan directions below, sitting with a graphic of the human body and its named parts beside me, I channeled the protocols of my teacher Jane Eckert, and of Kabat-Zinn and his colleagues Williams and Penman, adapting Kabat-Zinn's longer practice so that it is manageable even in busy routines. Eventually, you may want to listen to Jon Kabat-Zinn himself lead you through the scan on YouTube.[18]

It is important to set the scene for the scan. Find a quiet space. Resist hurrying. Eventually—I promise—as in mindful meditation, you will slip into the process naturally.

Find a comfortable position in a chair, sitting tall without slumping, bottom at the back of the chair, feet flat on the floor, hands in lap. Or lie flat on a bed, or mat, or floor, elevating head and knees until comfortable, with hands at your sides. (This is my preferred position, when time and place permit, and might be for you while you learn the process.)

The point of the scan is to breathe into distinct parts of the body, lingering over them, examining them systematically. (I linger over problematic parts, my ankle with its break repaired with metal pins, the lung tissue where the clot settled, my hard-of-hearing ears.)

After becoming practiced in the body scan, it is possible, in deep, focused moments, to bring the breath to pain, even the extreme discomfort of cancer treatment. We can breathe into sorrow. I have breathed into heartache, with some success. When I breathe into high anxiety or overwrought emotion, I breathe into my whole torso.

I spell out the routine below in its specificity, taking time with it even though the practice may seem obvious. Take comfort in mentally exploring the nooks and crannies of your body. Later, you can abbreviate the practice.

Let us follow the same plan that we did for meditative breathing. Devoting thirty minutes allows you to spend roughly three minutes on each of the ten parts of the scan. If you need to, repeat the scan until you internalize it. (This is a good activity for civility circles, where you can take comfort in the resonance of the group.)

Later, in the short form, we move through the scan in several minutes. Here we move slowly, meditating on our bodies themselves, what composes us, the substance of who we are. In the naming is the knowing; the naming brings parts into consciousness and gives us an opportunity to cherish the body that has brought us this far. We are calling out our substance, what composes our presence. This is the point of this meditation. So many of us are not really in touch with our bodies. Don't whiz through the process; enjoy the deliberation. Later, you can call up any part of the scan in moments of stress.

1. We follow Kabat-Zinn's practice of beginning at your feet and working upward. Continue deep, slow belly breathing. I like to rest my dominant hand on my belly, to be in touch with this measured breathing.

    Your feet deserve attention: they establish your stance; they have carried you to and fro for however many years. They allow you to stand tall. Breathe into them. Focus on their entirety. Then on their top, bottom, heels. Toes one at a time—big toes, all the way to the little toes, even examining the spaces between. Notice sensations such as tingling, numbness, callouses, or nothing at all. Focus on each foot separately, each for a moment. Return to your feet as a whole, and then notice how they connect to your ankles. On another in-breath, notice the ankles themselves, all around, registering sensations, accepting what is there.

2. Always moving up on an outbreath, move up the fibula and tibia of your lower legs to the patella of your knees, circling them, front, side, back, slowly, again to the front, noticing muscle groups, noticing what sensations are there, what tenderness, stiffness is there, or maybe nothing. As you breathe, be comfortable with what is there. You are claiming your body, sensing what it is, in the moment by moment of your scan. The point is to accept what you discover. Breathing regularly, move your attention up your thigh, along your femur, examining muscle groups that surround it, feeling their length, roundness, firmness, and fullness. Notice sensations you have not felt before.

3. On an outbreath, move your attention to the hip bones, to the ball-and-socket hip that joins with the femur, to the many muscles and nerves that move your legs and hips, to those broad bones that protect the pelvic area and that hold delicate internal organs. Notice the end of the vertebral column, focusing on what is there, breathing into it. The more focused you are, the more fruitful the scan will likely be.

4. Slowly, breathe into your lower torso, focusing on the lumbar area of the spine. Find those lower-level discs. Imagine spinal muscles, nerves, and tendons—all the time breathing deeply and slowly, lingering over your lower spine. Imagine the intricacies of bones, muscles, and tendons that support your back and that help support the weight of your body, the substance of you. Notice pressure points, and a nexus of pain, if any. Next focus on your lower back, then the intestinal area, with its organs so critical to your health. If your mind wanders, or wonders, return to your focus. Those thoughts are not you; they are clouds passing by.

5. On an outbreath, move up, slightly to waist level, and breathe into all that is there. You are at mid-point now.

I find my felt sense deep in this general area, the interior that is below my hand when it sits at my waist, with my fingers spread wide. I associate felt sense with embodied awareness. When I acknowledge such a thing as an interior knowing, a gut feeling, it originates here. I draw on my felt sense when I am centering myself, not only in meditation, but in thoughtful moments when I am searching for deep meaning of a concept, an interaction, a link between ideas or moments. These are also cognitive moments, but centering is a whole-body process, an embodied awareness, that, for me, seems to emanate from here. I locate a felt sense of civility here. This, too, is where the gut response of anger comes from. Mindful awareness can attenuate that anger.

6. Next breathe into your lungs, those vital organs that give the very breath you are using now, that move life-giving oxygen through your body. Focus on your rib cage, breathe into it, noticing it lift as you breathe, aware of your lungs, expanding contracting, expanding contracting, in the critical repetition that gives life. Linger over the breath in your lungs, as it fills your rib cage, and then relax.

As you settle into the second half of our process, acknowledge its deliberateness. Cherish your body. Cherish the process.

You give yourself over to massages and possibly skin treatments and grooming of your hair and nails. This inner practice, when you are mindfully comfortable with it and in tune with your body, will offer benefits beyond the physical.

7. Still moving to a new area on an outbreath, focus on your spine at the midpoint of your trunk, moving attention all the way up to the base of the skull and then all the way down to the coccyx. Breathe into your spine, as you move your focus from its bottom to its top: lumbar, thoracic, and cervical areas. Breathe into the support that the spine provides your body, especially the upper torso. Breathe into your posture, as when you stand tall. Sense its potential flexibility. Breathe into the protection your spine gives your spinal cords, and the nerves therein, your body's wiring. Breathe into the neurons, the nerve cells, communicating with receptors across your body. Focus intensely on any parts of your spine that feel vulnerable. On an in-breath, move to the midpoint of your spine.

8. On an outbreath, move your attention to your upper torso and feel your heart beating within, beating, beating, sending oxygenated blood through your body. Devote some time to this organ that is so symbolically significant of who you are, that is so central to your life itself, the organ no larger than the size of your fist. Contracting, relaxing. Vena cava, atrium, valves, ventricles, arteries, veins, aorta, blood, oxygen. Breathe life into all of these.

Imagine the "intelligence" of the heart as it operates in synchrony with your brain and the rest of the body. Acknowledge the coherence that exists between your heart and head, in tune with the rest of your body.

9. On an outbreath, realize how your arms extend from your shoulders. Notice the humerus, the long large bone that extends from the ball-and-socket shoulder joint to the elbow, the radius and ulna of your lower arm. Focus on problematic, possibly burning shoulder knots that connect, most certainly, to stress and the burdens you bear.

    Notice your hands, front and back, open and fist, knuckles and nails. Linger on your hands and fingers, as they are so essential in so many ways, vital in so many chores, reaching out in a handshake, connecting us to others, in civility. Linger on you thumb, the opposable thumb that allows your fingers to grasp objects, hugely important in our evolution from primates, from Lucy, our 3.2 million-year-old ancestor. Breathe into the possibility of reaching out to touch someone, or to grasp civility itself and hold it in your hands.

10. On an outbreath, move back up your arms to your shoulders and the top of your spine, where it meets your neck and balances your heavy head. When memories float in, let them pass, always returning to your breathing. Perhaps memories of "squaring your shoulders" as you faced a difficulty. Memories wisp by, but they are merely clouds passing over you for the moment, so brush them away and return to the particularity of your shoulders. Breathe into them.

11. On an outbreath, follow your spine up the back of your skull, breathing into its various parts. Explore the mechanisms of your eyes, ears, nose, and mouth, as well as the other parts of your face. Especially those ears through which you listen to the world. Next breathe into the various parts of the brain, this most complex part of the human body—the brain stem, the cerebrum, and the cerebellum.

    Finally, breathe into the presence of your integrative mind, supported as it is by the body and heart you have just scanned. Breathe into the image of your mind—its emergent + self-organized + embodied + relational powers, so necessary for civility.

12. Bring the scan to conclusion with another full body breath. On the inbreath—"I am;" on the outbreath—"civility."

You are now in a self-organized state of full awareness—strengths, weaknesses, aches, pains, such as they are. You have drawn on what Daniel J. Siegel calls the embodied mind. Further, in locating Gendlin's "felt sense of knowing," its properties may also be available to you.

Completing the body scan may, or may not be, cause for celebration the first time through. Its pure unfamiliarity may cause resistance. The process is mind-blowing for those who are not in touch with their bodies. Some are so incredibly tense that the work of the scan is very hard to do. Some relax so readily that they nod off and fall asleep, which is okay. Eventually, though, all of us have the potential to feel transported, as I and my classmates have, to a state of bodily awareness that sometimes approaches altered dimensions. Other times, the scan feels tedious. With repetition, though, the serenity of body awareness is restorative. The goal is to complete the scan often enough to get the feel of its completeness, its deep structure, slowly and deliberately, so that (any portion of) it is available in times of stress.

Why bother with this self-evident process? Mindfulness is a stepping stone to embodiment. The body scan is a way to feel ourselves as whole; if there is such a thing as embodying an idea, making it part of our very being, it will happen through the totality of awareness that mindfulness creates.

So, let us think of embodying civility. We ask, "Who am I?" We answer, "I am civility," not just theorizing it, not as in a mind trip, but of me, of my being. We have a felt sense of civility, we feel it as part of us. The body scan helps us achieve this awareness.

The Body Scan: Three-Minute Form

A real benefit of meditation is that is available to you anywhere, anytime. Having meditated deeply, the process is available to you anytime, anywhere. When you are feeling so stressed that concentration is difficult and the task in your day seems impossible, take three minutes for some bodyheartmindsoul breathing. Spend thirty seconds each moving in and out of your meditation, and two minutes in the heart of the scan.

1. Settle into a place and position where you are comfortable. You can do this at your desk. You may want to close your eyes as you center yourself. Move your harried breathing into the measured breathing of our meditations. Relax yourself into the presence you felt at the end of our meditations. You are being in and with your body.

2. Breathe into parts of your body, one at a time, pausing at those places that ache, that are vulnerable to the stress or angst you may feel, focusing your breathing there. Give yourself over to the meditation. Hands on your abdomen, and on an inbreathe, bring your attention to your feet, ankles, and legs. Then breathe into your hips, torso, and spine, from which nerves and muscles radiate. You are noticing the sensations in each of these places. Next breathe into your heart, slowing enough to be conscious of its beating. Then move onto your shoulders, arms, hands, and fingers, breathing into each of them. And, finally, breathe into your head and its interior.

3. Take another half-minute to move out of your meditation. To signal my humanity and to come out of deep focusing on my physicality, I do a short form of civility wings, mentally if I am in a public place, or simply one hand up from my side, briefly covering my heart, moving to the side of my head, and then up and around, as in a stretch, swooping humanity onto me. I am back in my world, calmer for the scan.

The practice can be abbreviated further. When I am in a state of incredible emotionality, I breathe into it, deeply and directly, for half a minute or so, as long as it takes for me to settle into a calmer state of mind. When I have learned something or heard something that shocks my being, I take measured breaths. This practice breaks the sense of loss and is an alternate to breaking down. It is also an alternate to thrashing out in hate or saying the nastiest thing you can think of.

The brief meditations are ever so more powerful when you have integrated the longer ones into your way of life. Doing so brings you to presence of mind so you can do the right thing.

The Wonder of Awareness

It is my hope for you that mindfulness practice will transport you to *wonder*, defined as "astonishment at something awesomely mysterious or new to one's experience."[19] The wonderfulness of mindful breathing and the body scan is such that, when integrated, they can be restorative. They contrast markedly from restorative practices like workouts, or visits to spas or salons. You literally take mindfulness practices with you; mindful

walking in a nature preserve is a glorious experience, why so many mindfulness retreats are held in beautiful settings.

We cannot escape our minds. Nor can we escape our bodies. As the
cliché goes, they are what they are, and we carry them with us. We long for
a harmonious working of all parts within them. Mindfulness practice,
with its sense of a greater whole, helps us to that awareness, which helps
us to civility.

Most of us tend to think of ourselves as the center of the universe, scientific reality aside. Deny it or not, life seems to be the experience of the
universe revolving around us in our daily comings and goings, with their
events, emotions, happiness, illnesses, challenges, and heartaches. Mindfulness centers us in this falderal, what Zorba calls the "full catastrophe,"
and gives us an opportunity to be aware of our bodies and take care of
them. When we slip into bodyheartmindsoul awareness, and find our
center, we understand how that moment is constituting us, and, understanding it, come to equanimity.

Think back to the signature which you appended to our civility pledge.
Recall that in our mindfulness meditations, our goal is to achieve awareness. Recall how mindfulness practice is bringing you to presence, the
demeanor of calm knowing, a manifestation of self-understanding, an
instantiation of a civil moment, a civil gesture, a civil action—the embodiment, the bodyheartmindsoul, of civility. Say to yourself, "I am civility."

Process #3
Listening Anew—
Toward Harmony

In the beginning is not the word. In the beginning is the hearing.
—Mary Daly

Having interrogated our identity and practiced mindful awareness, we now examine civility dynamics in the space around us. We want to examine the entirety of that space, to figure out what composes its resonance. So much of civility is carried in its reverberations, which sets in motion receptivity and reciprocity. Our goal is to listen anew, and we create an ambience for doing so by exploring all the happens in the space around us.

In working toward harmony, we bring our five senses to the fore—touching, tasting, smelling, seeing, and hearing. We are so comfortable with them that we barely notice all they do for us. Jon Kabat-Zinn suggests that we complicate our awareness by adding three more senses. Let us add mind as a sixth sense, that amazing combination of energy and information flow that absorbs all that is around us, organizing it so that it is consciously available to us, and subconsciously too, if we choose to plumb its rich depths. Through practicing mindfulness, we have come to understand that our mind—with its emergent, relational capacities—suffuses the space around us. A seventh sense, proprioception, allows us to be aware of what is going on around us, of the person behind us, of the noise off to one side, of the quality that allows parents to say to their children, "I have eyes in the back of my head!" And, finally, we add interoception—"the overall interior feel of the body as a whole"—that sense we explored so thoroughly in mindfulness practice.[1] Eight senses, really, all doing their work in the space around us. Some even say they can feel the vibrations of a momentous encounter. When our sensations work positively, we speak of their vibrancy. We call a person vibrant who resonates energy and life.

In examining these eight senses we become aware, of "elements of the environment through physical sensation," with attention to how those sensations are "interpreted in the light of experience."[2] In fact, theoretically speaking, we focus now, in this step of our journey to civility, on the interpretation of our sensations in light of experience. Perception takes center stage.

Much happens when that dynamism merges with the vibratory resonance of the space around us. We will enlist our relational mind in making the most of its resonance. Our sensate qualities resonate—our seeing, hearing, smelling, touching, tasting, thinking, noticing, and embodying—perceiving what goes on around us with our entirety. Think, for example, of all eight senses responding to the sight of a dear friend, or a favorite work of art, or a caress, or a kiss.

With our eight senses, we can read a situation. We are calling to attention all that happens with, in, and around our eight senses. In fact, we use one of those eight senses to mentally navigate our way through the space around us on the journey to civility.

Our goal is to bring harmony to the space we inhabit, this space in which we are always central. We bring to conscious awareness all that happens in this space, just as we brought conscious awareness to our body-heartmindsouls in mindfulness practice. With our senses fully operative, we bring this space alive. We use its vibrancy to best advantage, for the purposes of civility.

Let us imagine this space ever so carefully and breathe into it: imagine sweeping harmony into this space with civility wings, sending out full humanity to everyone, with similar potential to be mindfully present. This vibratory sending out and bringing in is the lifeblood of civility. It is within this space that our full humanity develops.

It is our intention to welcome the other into this space. Encountering the other is a sensory experience first and foremost: our eyes perceive skin tone and facial and bodily differences; ears hear new tonal dimensions in language sounds, even breathing sounds; noses detect scents and body odors; hands touch, fingertips sense skin calloused differently. The other's senses are doing the same.

Our minds are at work—ours and others,' all with the powerful quartet of our mind's qualities that we learned of in Process #2—emergent, self-organized, embodied, and relational—working the space around us. Resonance emanates—the awareness of life in all its permutations and complications. Our emotions swirl, too many to name: they consume us in love or, sadly, its opposite; in happiness or gloom; in enchantment or despair; in harmony or cacophony.

In the space around us resonates the unstated, the intangible. Body language. Sign language. Quiet, occasionally. Silence too, in its vast complexity. Silence, in verb form, as in to silence. Silence is voicelessness, sometimes enforced by traditions, often deliberate, as in the cases of women and of people of color in the United States and worldwide whose voices have been suppressed in so many ways over so many years.

The space of being silenced holds abuse. Women and men—victims of sexual harassment and predation—recounted on the national level how they were victims of the likes of Harvey Weinstein, Bill Cosby, Roger Ailes, Bill O'Reilly, and even priests, legislators, and presidents. Most sexual violence occurs at work, in public spaces, or at or near a person's home. Much of this violence never gets reported due to shame or fear of intimidation.

Violence is in the resonance of conflict, battles, and wars, small and large, to which the United States and other countries send troops and commit lives in attempts to bring some kind of satisfactory resolution. Those in Syria, Afghanistan, Iraq, Pakistan, Sudan, Somalia, Yemen, Nigeria, and most recently Niger, regularly make the nightly news, to say nothing of the wars of drug cartels in Central and South America. Kim Jong Un and Donald Trump, whose past actions suggest they have too few civil bones in their bodies, negotiate the most egregious exploitation of space possible with the threat of nuclear retaliation.

Yet our resonance on the personal level emanates: this is our personal power, we carry it with us, and it is contagious. In this space, in mindful awareness, our embodied, always emergent and relational brains see potential for civility. This space is our universe, one where we—and all of Earth's people in their spaces—may step back from struggle to rest. In this still space is now.

As citizens, we carry this potential in the moment by moment of our days. Our bodyheartmindsouls become capacious. We seize moments for civil change. No more othering. Make America kind again, one civil act at a time, in the moment by moment of our lives.

Space Invasion

Learned cultural factors and family practices determine when we feel our space has been invaded, whether by people, images, odors, noises, or vibrations of the digital landscape. Smart phones use that space in ways we wouldn't have imagined only a decade ago. They have taken a place alongside our senses in contemporary American society; they are ubiquitous technological extensions of our very hands, in our faces, tucked between chin and ear, resting on shoulder, neck craned. Doctors report seeing cases of neck and back pain caused by incessant looking down at cellphones.

The cost in psychic pain is also damaging. We have yet to understand how fully social media is transforming our society. Twitter influences national politics through outbursts that may well lack courtesy. Its informality moves so easily into sarcasm or insult. Indeed, social media short-circuits the understanding that comes from deep thought.

Cultural commentators analyze social media, its networking possibilities, its force of instantaneity, everything from cellphone addiction to cyberbullying to potential recruitment for global warfare—in the case of ISIS, using twenty-first century technology to support a seventh-century theology, or of Russians in 2016—to attempt to influence elections here and abroad.

When people learn I am writing on civility, they express distress about ways their space is invaded. Cellphones are only part of the problem. They resent perceived discourtesies, offensive language, or what they see as the in-your-face brashness of many social interactions, virtual or in person. They have many theories about where this behavior is so easily manifested.

Can we help people to better manners? To better ways of being? Yes, we can. We are taking the time and space of this book to connect courtesy to a new civility, to show that courtesy moves beyond manners and is embodied in our five processes.

The Good Vibrations of Resonance

All 7.6 billion people in our global village use each of their eight senses to make their way in the space around them, in villages, towns, cities, and open spaces—all part of our global village. Imagine the diversity of all sensate experiences!

Each of us occupies a place, has a fundamental right to have a space, and—a goal for a civil society—to have that space be safe. Let us think of ourselves in that space, with its inherent vibrancy, practicing civility and emanating peaceful vibes. When we feel anger, hate, exclusion, or any other negative emotions, we can take a mindfulness minute and own up to our prejudices and biases. We remember that emotions are bodily responses first and foremost, so we slow down and breathe into them. We feel our inbreath moving slowly to our toes, and then our outbreath moving up our bodies and out our nose and mouth, again and again. Thinking, "I am civility." Our three-minute body scan helps us to the state of resonance—body, heart, mind, soul, civility wings—where our mindfulness expands through good vibrations and brings space alive.

Now, through Process #3, we emanate harmony, so vital to the community-building impulse involved in creating civility. We know that positivity increases and prolongs good vibrations. A smile first, its facial muscles setting the positive tone, caring eye contact, pleasant greeting, hearty handshake. These are civility's gifts.

We also know things by their opposites, so let us also notice bad vibrations: the angry gesture, stiff posture, fixed frown, glaring eyes, braced shoulders, arms and shoulders closed in, resigned sigh, grimace. These vibrations are nearly impenetrable.

Finding Grace in the Space around Us

It is no stretch for us to infuse vibrations with grace. *Grace* is a disposition to be generous or helpful; it conveys a sense of goodwill, a sense of fitness, or propriety. We find an abundance of grace in meditative practices of Eastern traditions and from most religious leaders and their congregants and from health professionals.

I have found grace in the librarians who locate books from libraries far away, who take my requests, and every other patron's, seriously, explaining in soft, caring voices when the book will arrive. I find it in the local bookstore café where people get their coffee and tasties and move quietly to tables where they chat over books and magazines. I find it in public parks and gathering places where people go to relax in comfortable, lovely surroundings.

We find it in prayer. In the community service activities of churches. In the gracious volunteerism that contributes so mightily to social and health causes. So, let us infuse grace into the space around us. Civility itself has a quality of grace. A civil act is generous, helpful, conveys a sense of goodwill, considers the fitness of behavior to the occasion, and respects proprieties. We will demonstrate the generosity and goodwill of grace through artful listening. But first let us explore the nuances of silence.

All Silence Has Meaning

Silence—the unspoken—is a rhetorical act that can be as powerful as the spoken or written word. Like speech, the meaning of silence depends on a power differential that exists in every rhetorical situation: who can speak, who must remain silent, who listens, and what those listeners can do.
—**Cheryl Glenn**

Of one thing we can be certain: silence is not an absence.

In our identity interrogation and mindfulness meditation, the subject of silence has been tacit—unexpressed yet present. In interrogating our identity, we studied power dynamics, asking: Have we been silenced? Have we silenced? Has there been a time when silence was healing? When has silence brought understanding and possibly a desire for common cause?

Silence is at the heart of meditation, so we bring knowledge of its richness to the vibratory awareness we are developing here. We are already sensing, quoting Glenn again, that "[s]ilence itself is not silent: it is the origination of sound, the sound or creative flow of being (bodies being beating bodies, fires being crackling fires, rain being pattering rain, computers being humming computers, and so on)."[3]

You may have experienced what Glenn calls "the creative flow of being" in either your meditative breathing or your body scan, when you are listening to the sound of your body or when you are in tune with your felt sense. There is no passivity in this kind of silence; there can be alertness, sensitivity, attentiveness, and sometimes stoicism. Indeed, your own silence can allow other voices to be heard.[4] Yet silence is sometimes an "imbalance,....[when it is] weakness, impotence, fear, and subordination in the face of dominance."[5]

What we are really doing here is exploring vibrations and sorting out what kind we will carry on our civility journey. We begin with attentiveness and sensitivity to what is happening in the silence around us. Our sensitivities locate and open up silences. Our dictum: all silence has meaning.

Developing Artful Listening

How do we listen? How do we demonstrate that we honor and respect the person talking and what the person is saying? How do we translate listening into language and action, into the creation of an appropriate response?

—Jacqueline Jones Royster

Welcome to the art of listening class.

Imagine listening to help others be "well-heard" as an end in itself. Life as we know it would change.

Listening well is a civil, intentional—and artful—act. When you hear, you are an artist, creating the space in which you receive sound, and doing what you will with those sound vibrations you translate to language. Listening is highly personal. Two listening spaces are never identical. Nor is listening stable. It is always contextual. Just as the act of listening is constantly changing, so is what is being said, who is speaking, the gist of conversation, and, thinking even more expansively, language itself.

Given all this, imagine for a moment: there is as much to be gained from effective listening as there is from effective speech. Imagine devoting as much time and energy to listening as you do to speech. Steven Covey, author of 7 *Habits of Highly Effective People*, says we don't listen to hear but rather to respond. In giving listening its fair share of attention, we emerge as artists of listening. As we breathe new life into listening, we breathe it into civility.

So why is listening so underappreciated? Is it because success is associated with outgoing confidence, a bright personality, and speaking up and out? Susan Cain, in *Quiet: The Power of Introverts in a World That Can't Stop*

Talking, explains how our country's most prestigious business schools emphasize outgoingness, verbosity, and a space-consuming confidence. Calm composure that emanates knowingness is less valued.

It is discriminatorily assumed that men talk and women listen: talk is associated with the masculine and valued positively, and listening with the feminine and valued negatively. The assumption carries over to the professions, business boards, and leadership positions, where men still dominate. Gender, race, and class biases play into the narrative described above and "allow" the privileged to listen with less care than the underprivileged, the privileged assuming a casualness that less privileged cannot dare to.

In any case, listening surely joins the work of the other senses as they shape our identity and mindful awareness. Careless listening is often to blame for the biases we uncovered in our identity interrogation. You've surely heard the familiar refrain: people hear what they want to hear. Not listening well—or deliberately tuning someone out—shows the disrespect of discrimination.

Here, bringing vibratory resonance to the fore, we tease out the possibilities and potentials of listening well. Think of physical therapy classes that build our core by strengthening parts of our bodies that are out of balance and need repair. The listening lessons that follow strengthen our civility core. The therapies strengthen our intention to recreate ourselves as civil beings. They are part and parcel of civility composure, and we now add them to identity fairness and mindful awareness.

You are poised for the artistry of listening well. Remember: In the beginning is not the word. In the beginning is the hearing.

Turning Artful Listening into Action

[O]nce we have a vocabulary for explaining what we do when we listen, it is easier to convince others to listen the way we do—and to change the way we listen ourselves.
—Peter Rabinowitz

Listening well is absolutely critical in mediation, negotiation, conflict resolution, and reconciliation—processes that occur on the road to personal, local, national, and international peacemaking. To get to artistry in listening, we examine listening's cognitive, experiential, and sensate properties. I draw my approach from personal experience and a lifetime of awareness and study. Ironically, my father's instruction to all seven of us kids to be seen and not heard probably helped all of us learn to be good listeners.

My thinking also draws on the scholarship of two women who are transforming the field of rhetoric by focusing on "silence and listening as rhetorical acts"—Cheryl Glenn, whom you have already met, and Krista Ratcliffe, author of a book on rhetorical listening that we will turn to later. These authors not only define listening's complexities, but also insist that helping people be "well-heard" is an avenue to social change. It is also an avenue to civility.

As always, we strive to integrate these processes into our civil being. Now and then as you go through your day, inhale slowly, then exhale, tracing the breath up, down, and up your body. Hold it in your hearing. Realize these two processes—the hearing and the listening that follows—as civil social action, bringing them into your consciousness.

Listening adds another dimension to our breathing, hearing the body's complexity in the moment by moment of breathing in, breathing out, understanding that artful listening has healing power in a family, neighborhood, or country riven by misunderstandings, anger, and hatred.

Listening also adds a rich dimension to our vision, in the sense that vision is limiting because we can only see what our eyes are looking at. Theorist Martin Jay calls it sight bias, or ocular-centrism: "as one object is foregrounded, other objects blur, fade into the background, fall outside the field of vision."[6] We can sometimes hear what we literally cannot see, focused as our field of vision is on our gaze. Screeching tires. Gunshots. Action in storytelling. Here we put listening in the foreground, to help us "see" more clearly.

The five ways of listening I describe below are interwoven and nuanced—active, say back, contemplative, compassionate, and accountable. I conclude with accountable listening because the situational demands of finding common ground absolutely require accountability.

Active Listening

We must remember that one of the most insidious ways of keeping women and minorities powerless is to . . . let them speak freely and not listen to them with serious intent.

—Mitsuye Yamada

When listening actively, we "listen with serious intent" to what the speaker is saying, rather than listening noncommittally, with divided attention, or not at all. This approach can build rapport, and—more importantly—trust, because the speaker knows the listener is genuinely acknowledging, or gathering in, what the speaker is saying. The speaker recognizes active listening because they can detect from the listener's bodily responses and cues that active listening is underway. It follows that active listening implies a response that affirms the listener's understanding.

I am getting directions on how to do chores. In the kitchen with mother, I learn to prepare meals, launder clothes, clean the kitchen, harvest, clean, can green beans and tomatoes, and make scrumptious pies that earned an A for my 4-H project. In the process, my listening is accompanied by mother's explanation and demonstration. Her voice and my sight dominate, listening taken for granted, not seeming to call for the focused attention of show and tell.

"Pay attention to what I'm telling you," mother would say. "Are you listening? I don't want your fingers to get sliced." Or, "This is how you do it right. Watch, I will show you again."

The ante is upped when I might be in danger. I listen to my mother tell me to keep my fingers and the utensils out of the beaters as I make chocolate chip cookies for my first-grade class. I follow brother Jim's instructions to keep my fingers safe when I feed ears of corn into the shelling machine, the kernels to be food for our flock of chickens.

My bodily cues show I am listening. I lean in, furrow my brows, concentrate, affirming that I hear. I demonstrate my understanding by completing the task myself, the first few times with some demonstrative coaching. I listen actively, and my success making cookies and shelling corn is proof that I have listened well. I can see and touch and smell the cookies and the corn. I have heard, the hearing/listening fading into the reality of the accomplishment, the hearing/listening folding into doing—the seeing, touching, smelling. Tasting the cookies, feeling the texture of the corn rough in my hands. Active listening has been central to completing the task. It is understood to be part of the process.

In this scenario, I, the active listener, pay close attention to what my mother and brother, the speakers, are saying, not noncommittally, nor with divided attention. Mom and Jim know I am genuinely listening through my body's response, through my smile, eye contact, and body language. I understand. I will get it right. I have listened actively.

"Say back" is an extension of active listening. I ask the listener to "say back" to me what I have just said in their own words. This sounds simple but involves the complex cognitive response of hearing, understanding, formulating that understanding into words that summarize, and stating the formulation in such a way that reflects understanding. Not so simple after all.

Increasing the complexity of the task increases the possibility of misunderstanding. It is exactly this possibility that calls for say-back.

Say back how you go about shelling the corn. Please, say back to me what time and where it is, I will pick you up after your music lesson. Say back what you are to bring from the store. Can you review my suggestions for solving this problem with your classmate?

Say-back is an effective tool in any form of intense discussion, as a way of slowing the pace, and pausing to assess where all parties to the discussion are in their thinking: "Now, where exactly are we in this discussion?" I used the phrase often in my years in the classroom. We will further explore the use of say-back in our compassionate listening segment.

Notice how you listen throughout your day. Then turn to your journal and reflect on what you observed about yourself as listener. In what circumstances did you listen actively? What motivated you to do so? What was gained in doing so? Who and what got ignored when you were not actively engaged in listening? How did it feel when you were not listened to? To what do you attribute an other's failure to listen? Was that failure possibly attributable to your gender, race, class, or age? Is your own motivation to listen attributable to any of those markers? Have you noticed who gets listened to most readily, and in what circumstances. In attending to these intricacies, you are extending your listening repertoire. Your very act of listening anew leads to harmonious exchanges. In listening anew, you create harmony anew.

Contemplative Listening

While say back is listening for public purposes, contemplative listening is deep, unhurried listening for self-reflection, in preparation, possibly of a response. It is for the self, although not necessarily self-centered. We listen contemplatively to get to harmony, ultimately for the sake of reasoning well, whereas in meditative listening, we listen simply to be with and of ourselves; thoughts are simply clouds floating by.

This kind of thinking is an interior process. The mind contemplates what is heard and thinks it through. We affirm sight, taste, touch, and smell in exteriority, in plain sight. But can others tell you really are hearing, really listening? Not so much. Only if you signal through body language. Parents repeat the familiar, "Are you listening to me?" The hearing hoped for, the listening hard to tell. Women and other minorities have long known that this privacy of listening, and its intricate connection with the mind, allows them at least a degree of freedom in response and planning, even in the face of verbal, or physical, onslaught. Indeed, as we contemplate, we figure out what we hear really means for ourselves, perhaps for what we believe, for action we intend to take. In this case our contemplation is proactive: we listen to assimilate, to make sense of ourselves and our circumstances; we listen to reason. Looking forward, Process #5 on reasoning well offers two ways to contemplate the chain of reasoning as it unfolds through listening. The ultimate focus is outward, the inner process yielding insight for action in your world.

Contemplative listening is about slowing down, being comfortable in silence itself. For example, the restorative power of listening in Quaker worship services is thought to transfer to Quaker life itself. In their services Quakers become attuned to silence, finding a centered place where the mind becomes quiet, where they listen for wisdom, for the still, small voice of God, for a sense of the sacred, which they are to carry into their lives on a day-to-day basis. In their services they learn to be comfortable in silence, to go deep to their centers, listening beyond words, to the source of power within themselves. As they listen in communion with others, there may be an assimilation of soulful vibrations that further guides them through their days.

I bring contemplative listening to Universalist Unitarian Church services, to settings of reverence (recent funerals of young nieces and my favorite teacher), to tea with my sister when I sit on her patio next to the park listening to birds, and to book clubs, fiction and nonfiction. On walks on nature trails, contemplative listening can merge with meditation.

Compassionate Listening

One of the tasks of true friendship is to listen compassionately and creatively to the hidden silences. Often secrets are not revealed in words, they lie concealed in the silence between the words or in the depth of what is unsayable between two people.
—John O'Donohue

The goal is to anchor . . . listeners . . . in our core (rather than our defenses), inviting others to do the same. Ideal Compassionate Listening is completely nonjudgmental and nonreactive; the listener is not persuaded by the speaker's words but maintains his or her own ideas without feeling threatened by the presence of the other's [ideas]. In this way, listeners model for the speakers how to move beyond their defenses and advocacy in order to speak from the heart. If people can speak and listen in non-oppositional ways with the goal of understanding one another, change becomes possible.
—Joy Arbor

Let us add the humane emphasis of compassion to our listening repertoire in preparation for our emphasis on accountability. We will employ say back and contemplative listening in the process.

We are in awareness, engaging mindfully, conscious of the strength of compassionate composure. We listen anew, alert to and identifying with the (perhaps) emotional and (perhaps) unfamiliar aura and message of the speaker. Our own aura projects inclusivity, an openness we hold even as we see and hear the reprehensible; in civility, after all, we search for footholds to common decency.

We have no trouble coming up with examples of shutting down altogether or outrageously exploding—or any behavior in between—over long-held resentments and differences of opinion. How difficult it is to put aside outrage, even simple disagreement, and to let the words and their meaning lie there for examination. There is no magic to get us through this moment. How often I've thought, "If I can just be civil, I can get through this mess." Figuring out the mess certainly a motivation for writing this book.

Listening compassionately to a person we don't agree with is sometimes hard work, as in the example below. One of the most compelling examples I know is Joy Arbor's participation in the Compassionate Listening Project's citizen delegation to Israel/Palestine. She and others in her group feel anguish while listening to a Palestinian tell stories of suffering in the Israeli occupation. Arbor explains:

> Compassionate Listening, a model of listening across difference that highlights the humanity rather than the political positions of the other in order to effect long-term social change, provides theories and practices for listening across difference that complement and complicate [any] inquiry into listening.[7]

Listening compassionately is challenging, immensely so, as you may well be listening for multiple purposes and to abhorrent ideas, jarring injustices, emotional upheavals, or long-held resentments. You will be listening to (in)humane matters in which you may very well have been a participant, in which case your emotions run rampant. Say back can possibly resurrect you from this emotionality.

I have been in such moments myself. They stay with us, possibly forever. We ruminate. There is emotional damage. Relationships are damaged. Rather than let this damage fade as unresolved, deconstruct the circumstances according to the compassionate and accountable procedures below. Doing so might keep you from playing the record over and over again, and help you clarify and integrate the experience(s) so that you can come to some kind of peace with them. If you can so do, you move toward full humanity.

Further, real-life altercations proceed so rapidly that compassionate listening seems nearly impossible. The best we can do is internalize a process so that it can come to the fore to slow an exchange and attenuate emotion. Who ever said being compassionate is easy?

This process is not one of listening quietly and then secretly holding grudges. It is putting yourself out there for the possibility of change. In our constructed case below, we sense the relief the Palestinian feels at being well-heard. Hearing well includes the intention to change.

I adapt the steps from Arbor's description of the compassionate listening project below.[8] As you read, imagine yourself in such a humane experience. Look especially at how compassion evolves. Remember too the amazing quartet of qualities of mind that helps this compassion along: its embodied, self-organized, emergent, relational qualities. Remember too Siegel's dictum that meaning emerges in relationships. In other words, our minds are suited for compassion.

Recall that here we are emphasizing the personal over the political; one's humanity is emphasized first and foremost. Arbor tells us there will be triggers—"those emotional responses in your body, stomach, and heart that make [you as listener] want to jump in and respond to another's stories, ending listening." A common behavior is to go to the extreme—to shut down in the face of dissension, or to raise the level of discourse from reason to rant. Arbor explains that "these triggers show us which ideas, positions, and stories provoke our defenses." She clarifies, "The goal is not to ignore one's triggers but to recognize the moments when one has reacted or experienced changes in one's body that impede listening, note them, and gently refocus attention on the speaker."

We see that compassionate listening is also humane listening. The steps are described below:

1. The speaker tells a personal story, likely one of not having been well understood. In the telling, the speaker may notice, possibly for the first time, through the saying, connections between and among his or her own experiences and positions; listeners may notice connections between the speaker's experience and their own. This story, as stories so often do, helps listeners relate to or connect with the speaker's humanity.

2. Listeners engage in contemplative listening. Then, in Arbor's words, they "mirror what they have heard from the speaker, in order to make the speaker feel 'well-heard'." In being listened to, the speaker experiences what Arbor rightly says may seem something of a miracle—a non-oppositional method of engaging with people across difference, conveyed through good vibrations.

3. The listeners, on the other hand, "hold themselves open" in order to "make sense of" stories very different from their own. Such magnificent promise in the phrase "Hold ourselves open to possibility," a promise we know from Daniel J. Siegel that our mind can deliver on.

Civility composure and its quiet, mindful breathing help to tame triggers and "hold ourselves open" to opposing or different ideas.

1. Again, following Arbor's sequence, listeners "say back," thanking speakers for what they have heard, even if they disagree with it, continuing their summary until the speaker feels "well heard," until there is agreement on what has been intended and said. These exchanges are the heart of compassionate listening.

2. Finally, there is inquiry, or strategic questioning, that assumes some kind of action will follow. For example, Arbor suggests we ask, "What might we do to address this problem?" Questions are designed to open up options and allow participants to rethink their ideas.

Imagine yourself engaging in such a profound, humane experience. Internalize the steps so that you can listen compassionately in the next contentious situation you face. The speaker feels well heard, listeners hold themselves open in order to make sense, listeners notice triggers that impede listening yet stay with the speaker, listeners say back, listeners inquire about possible actions to be taken, and Q&A opens up options for response. Practice, practice, practice this process until you internalize it.

We have had initial practice with this approach to compassionate listening in our identity interrogation when we asked of ourselves, "What have I learned from this experience? How can I change my behavior? How can I forego discrimination? How can I make the transformation to civility? What actions will follow my insights?"

When we have fully sustained compassionate listening, especially on topics about which we feel strongly and hold differing views, we are embodying an ideal—the best we can be in a state of dissension. We are embodying civility, on the road to peacemaking, embodying full humanity.

Accountability Listening

[G]enuine listening, with an accountability logic and the intent to change one's own rhetoric . . . gives American citizens a huge responsibility—to practice the kind of discourse . . . that can help us to find a common ground in the public sphere.

—Joyce Middleton

Remember the caution: stop, look, and listen before you cross the street. Listening occurs at the end of the triplet, emphasizing the possibility of hearing what we cannot see. It is that possibility that we are exploring here: hearing what we cannot see.

In doing so, we expand active, compassionate listening to listening accountably, which has more complicated cognitive demands than active listening, and listening to say back. Here we listen with an intent to reason and respond in an accountable way, and with a possibility of changing one's own thinking, words, and responses—and acting on the change. Rhetorician Krista Ratcliffe calls this "rhetorical listening," which she describes in her book of the same name.[9]

With accountable listening comes a huge responsibility: a commitment to internalize the words and meaning of another, as you understand them through your practices of active, compassionate listening, and to welcome that understanding—not necessarily adopting the understanding yourself but still acknowledging it—as part of your own being, and hence your thinking and actions.

Striving for civility asks a lot of us, and no act is more central than the one described above—the commitment to listen well, absorb the words, consider them, give them due regard, offer understanding if not agreement, and take appropriate action on that understanding. We are listening to the depths of our very being, with the intent of acting with civility.

I am helped to this kind of bodyheartmindsoulful listening through an image that leads us to actionable behavior—understanding as standing under, as Ratcliffe spells out. The Standing-Under Listening graphic provides a visual summary. As a first step, you will be standing under words as they wash over you. A glance at the graphic allows you to visualize the process and soak up the words.

Ratcliffe uses the term *discourse* to refer to the various meanings we carry with us from spoken and written texts. The term is handy here because its broadness has the potential to capture all that is going on in an incivility.

In our hypothetical case, Ratcliffe asks the listener to absorb everything that goes on in a heated exchange—she refers to these exchanges as "texts" of the various stories we tell and the "records" we play.

She explains:

Standing under discourse means letting discourses wash over, through, and around us and then letting them lie there to inform our politics and ethics ...

[We must] listen ... to hear and imagine how these discourses might affect not only ourselves but others. ...

Standing under discourses does not guarantee agreement ... ; it does, however, present a possibility of hearing what we cannot see. ...[10]

STANDING-UNDER LISTENING
FOR UNDERSTANDING, STAND UNDER WORDS
LET THEM WASH OVER, THROUGH AND AROUND YOU

What has been said or written

Desires and dreams

Discord and differences

Unconscious presences and absences

What is unstated but relevant

What is fuzzy, not clear

Both speaker and listener

* Realize and acknowledge their own fluid and
particular standpoints

* Imagine how these words, in their various forms,
affect others as well as themselves

* Let what has been said and absorbed stay with them,
to inform their next actions, their politics,
their ethics, their civility

Adapted from Krista Ratcliffe, *Rhetorical Listening.* Illustration by Susan Panning.

The standing-under image is resonant with the vibrations of the space around us. The image brings our "listening" mind to more than our own self-interested desires. In the process, we focus on the implications of our exchanges, in their entirety, in their emotionality. Ratcliffe tells us that "the goal of understanding is a broader cultural literacy within which we may negotiate our daily attitudes and actions, our politics and our ethics."[11]

Let us describe the process of standing under, just as we have conceptualized compassionate listening. You will notice the similarities, the most profound of which is, to repeat, an intentionality, not just to listen but to take the listening to heart in order to act on it, to be accountable.

Ratcliffe describes the following actions, delineated in the graphic (emphasis mine):

- Conceptualize understanding as standing under;
- Think of *discourse* as what is spoken or written in the past or present;
- Listen with undivided attention and let words and all that they mean wash over you, holding on to what is said;
- Consciously stand under [what is spoken] and *recognize the many strands of thinking within it*, realizing these words may be based on what has been said or written in the past;
- Listen carefully, for *desires, dreams, discord, and differences* that underlie the message;
- Realize these discourses surround not only us but others who may be listening as well;
- Acknowledge our standpoints, which may very well differ from those being stated;
- Listen for (un)conscious presences, absences, and unknowns —what is not being said, what is unstated but relevant, what motivations are present but unstated, what is fuzzy and doesn't seem clear;
- Listen to imagine how the discourses might affect others;
- Let them stay with you to inform your own very next actions, as well as the politics and ethics you adopt in your efforts after civility.

In summary, standing under these discourses means acknowledging their existence, and consciously integrating this slew of hot-wired information into our worldview and decision making. Thank you, Krista Ratcliffe, for this conceptualization, so essential to the practice of civility.

You will be wise to embed the "standing-under words/words washing over" imagery in your listening mind, for it captures the words, emotions, desires, dreams, discords, and complexities of contention.

You will find the potential for civility in the fluidity of words washing over you, as you stand under them. The image is spiritual, as in being bathed by words, possibly cleansed by them as their full meaning is absorbed, as being cleansed of the animosity of incivility.

Standing under is still another way of unpacking a situation through intense, thoughtful listening—listening in full humanity, aware of the speaker's interdependence with us, finding threads that can lead to common ground.

Practice standing-under listening as you go through your days, letting words wash over you as you encounter conversations or situations that are antithetical to your own identity.

Stand under one of your own most daunting stories of othering, perhaps one of exclusivity, one you owned up to in our identity interrogation. One that, in memory, pierces your bodyheartmindsoul for its incivility. One you would take back if only you could. You may have analyzed it in your journal already or talked it over with a friend in a civility circle. Let us assume there is still more to be understood about its genesis and delivery.

Stand under this story you might have buried and listen for its various strands of meaning. Krista Ratcliffe tells us that embedded in these stories will be themes, events, ideas, words, beliefs, and actions that you find disagreeable or even abhorrent. Retrieve moments of prejudice from your own repertoire of incivilities—we all have them—and, with graphic at hand, work your way through the many strands of meaning that comprise the discourse.

Ratcliffe tells us to listen to ourselves with undivided attention and intention to understand. (In scholarly terms, both the attention and the intention are rhetorical, part of meaning-making.) Let us understand the standing-under image as an effort to be accountable, to be responsible, and to change one's action as a result. We want to get past the angst, emotion, and confusion, to knowing. We are hearing what we cannot see. We are tuning in to the resonances in the space around us.

Standing under expands our listening zone: we stand under the abundance of memories, images, feelings, and emotions that wash over us.

We are expanding the concept of listening: rest assured, when stories wash over us, stories that clash with our experiences, norms, or dearly held religious or political beliefs, there will be a visceral response, born in molecules of emotion, in our very cells, in our very identity, affecting our physiology—and we will need to call on every ounce of fairness and awareness to listen responsibly, as words wash over us.

Imagine ourselves, standing under the shower of mental and bodily "discourses," in the past and present, as we move though the challenges of our days. Are we standing under them so that we absorb them and feel them as our own, as in our example of compassionate listening above? Are we seeing ourselves as others see us? Have we, as Ratcliffe suggests, "invite(d) the desires of others into our consciousness and accord(ed) these desires a place in which to be heard?"

We are calling on the mind's amazing ability for nuance as words wash over us.

> I go to a memory of exclusivity in my first year at Baldwin Wallace College (now University)—not once inviting the two black women who lived next door into my own room for conversation. Oh, I offered the usual pleasantries. In this standing-under moment of exclusion from my black dorm mates, I sense my posture stiffen, some tenseness, an excuse—and I knew it was an excuse—that there was no space in my life of classes, studying, cafeteria waitressing, English Department office work, boyfriends, chitchat, and sorority life, to carve out space for them. I settled for less, as did so many in that day—a friendly demeanor but a closed space, a nod to caring about black people, but no actionable behavior in support of the caring. I stand under an anguished desire to be able to live these exchanges again, in fairness, in awareness, in resonance and harmony, in civility. Ultimately, there were daily acts of exclusivity, of not-so-veiled racism, from my perch of white privilege. In this example, I stand under the cumulative discourse of my personal behavior with shame.

I have brought into my being what had been so naturalized before, as Ratcliffe says, that it was not visible.

To bring into your own being what has been so naturalized that it was not visible, turn to your journal and follow the prompts in the account-ability worksheet below. How can we help others to civility if we do not do the hard work of self-examination in order to be accountable? My shame was palpable as I wrote the account above. I take no solace in knowing that I was not alone in my behavior. This acknowledge-ment of our prejudicial behavior is part of the process of coming to fairness, bringing the injustice to awareness, hitting the right notes to create harmony, to create civility. Proceeding tenderly, tell the sto-ries you must, letting words wash over you, attuned to their nuances, for personal accountability. In telling these stories, you approach full humanity.

Civility as Process

I remember my mother saying, "He should hear himself talk," when a loving but tiresome uncle came to visit, the one who held forth without pause and with prejudice, always with a smelly cigar, the one who claimed food prepared by a black maid at his cousin's home left him nauseous.

Mother was on to standing-under listening. At the very least, mother's homily raised our consciousness. If our uncle had been insightful enough to listen to himself talk, or we had been brave enough to assist him in doing so, how might all of us have changed? In remembering to hear our-selves talk we are not only listening sensitively but also consciousness-raising for accountability.

Recall Mary Daly's words: "In the beginning was not the word. In the beginning is the hearing." In other words, we are human beings first. We are bodyheartmindsouls first, hearing, words washing over us. Their res-onances are absorbed in our contextual and relational minds, positioned to help us figure our way to civility.

We are at a critical juncture. Let us summarize. It is our intention to be civil, in the here-and-now moments of our lives. In asking "Who am I?" we have scanned our identity, and owned it by integrating it to get to at fairness.

Through mindfulness meditation, we bring awareness to succeeding moments of now. With civility tools inherent in awareness, we bring incipient civility into the resonant harmony of the space around us. Our brilliant systemic bodyheartmindsouls retrieve the possibility of civility in ongoing moments of now.

Ultimately, if we bring our felt sense of this process, with its incipient civility, to our everyday lives, we can bring our bodyheartmindsoulful beings to negotiations for common cause. We can find common ground.

Standing Under Memories
for Civility Accountability

Identify an incivility—one of some proportion and consequence—that you'd take back if you could. Stand under each or any of the following that may have been at issue, and jot a few words of association, to get at understanding and accountability. You are reconstructing a story that seems so naturalized as not to be visible—perhaps the origins of a feud, a buried incident that embodies racism, misogyny, ageism, gender prejudice, and so on. Analyze according to the dimensions explained in Process #3.

Desires _____   Themes _____

Dreams _____   Events _____

Discord _____   Ideas _____

Differences _____   Words _____

Beliefs _____

Mood _____

Impulses _____

Other free associations _____

Replay, or reenact the story above within a framework of civility accountability, using our technique of standing-under listening, to be accountable:

Desires _____   Themes _____

Dreams _____   Events _____

Discord _____   Ideas _____

Differences _____   Words _____

Beliefs _____

Mood _____

Impulses _____

Other free associations _____

Describe a prescient moment when you invited another's "discourse," or story, into your consciousness and allowed its inherent desires to be heard.

Suggestions for Journal Entries and Civility Circle Activities

Add harmony to your meditation routine. Meditate, imagining four identity markers—gender, race, religion, and politics—embodied in a best sense of your civil self. Embrace standing-under listening to capture all that is comprised in a moment of exchange.

> Breathe into the good vibrations of your resonance. Listen to your breath. Hear your breath, recognizing that the being precedes the hearing. Breathe into hearing itself, and the listening it allows. Imagine artful listening. Know artful listening is active listening. Meditate on listening as pure pleasure; when contemplative listening brought insight; when listening brought you and others compassion; and when listening accountably helped you realize an intention. Listen to your bodyheartmindsoul. Breathe into your mind itself, and then into its amazing capacities—its self-organized, embodied qualities, its emergent, relational qualities. Imagine good vibrations through civility wings as you pull humanity to you, in its diversity, and in its interdependence. In those vibrations is a mood that encapsulates greater good. Breathe into common ground. Think: I am a calm, relaxed, nurturing listener. Imagine listening as devotion, evocative of soul, extending into the space around you.

Repeat regularly. Careful listening takes practice, as does meditation itself.

Recall and explain a time when each of the following kinds of listening played a role in your life: say back, contemplative listening, compassionate listening, and accountability listening.

Remember an occasion of silencing and describe its repercussions for you, positive and negative.

Undertake a Quaker-like experience of discernment in listening. "Only listen" to allow yourself to "Only connect . . ." (in the epigraph to E. M. Forster's *Howards End*), to tune into intuition, to the consciousness of civility.

Process #4
Developing Empathy—
Toward Compassion

I am suggesting that we do not see only the direct possibilities for becoming better than we are when we struggle toward the reality of the other. We also have aroused in us the feeling, "I must do something." When we see the other's reality as a possibility for us, we must act to eliminate the intolerable, to reduce the pain, to fill the need, to actualize the dream. When I am in this sort of relationship with another, when the other's reality becomes a real possibility for me, I care.
—**Nel Noddings**

Caring is an emotional dynamic that brings civility to life.

Caring is a social dynamic that makes life worth living.

Caring as we are defining it here is more than a simple, neutral display of concern. As citizens in search of civility we are activists in search of transformation, so neither our demeanor nor behavior is neutral. The scholar Ibram X. Kendi warns against "taking comfort in a false neutrality of being 'not racist'," asserting that people are either racist or anti-racist.[1] Our caring concern does not "take comfort in a false neutrality" that is devoid of committed action. Our caring is dynamic, active, full of energy and devoted to full humanity of us all.

We humans are not by nature social isolates. We long to connect with others. We long to care and be cared for. When we care and are cared for, we feel we belong, we feel connected. In being cared for, we learn to receive and acknowledge care, and then to respond with caring. We build relationships one by one—a premise for *Creating a New Civility*.

A commitment to caring has underpinned our study all along. We looked first at ourselves, at naming our identities and getting them in touch with our bodyheartmindsouls, for the ultimate purpose of civil interactions. We put our senses to work in the space around us, attuning them as we relate to others. Here we study relationships themselves. We want to connect with others in civility. We add another dimension to our journey to civility. We will increase our capacity to empathize.

Even though caring seems natural, something we already know a lot about, it is worthwhile to apply our civility lens to its dynamics. When we ask of ourselves, "Who am I?" the underlying assumption is that we are humane, seeking fairness. When we undertake mindful meditation, we also think of ourselves as humane, as one with the universe, at peace with ourselves in ongoing moments of now. When we scan our senses, focusing particularly on hearing, we listen out of a humane concern for understanding. An intention to care underpins our work.

Yet it seems useful to push ahead and ask, "What does it mean to care?" What does caring really look, smell, sound, taste, and feel like? What do we do when we care?

We are not speaking of care here as suffering of mind or mental anguish, although we recognize that at times caring becomes burdensome. Nor are we discussing the profession of providing social or medical care, although the caring we discuss here informs its work. We will not specifically address the huge, important, separate area of caregiving for the ill and infirm, although some of our principles apply.

We will not examine aesthetical caring for things and ideas, although an aesthetical quality most likely suffuses the caring relationship, as well as the civil relationship.

Nor are we speaking of caring in the romantic, passionate sense, although, the qualities named here serve romantic relationships well. We are addressing specific caring relationships in the day-to-day occasions in which we interact with those whom we meet in our lives. These qualities will serve you well as you seek to achieve full humanity and to put grudges, long-held animosities, and possibly even prejudices aside.

As always, our approach is humanist and functionalist in that our concepts—in their workable emphases on civil behavior—help civility thrive. In adding compassion to fairness and awareness and harmony, we continue to full humanity.

As always, we go to work on the local level. Yet we hold in mind what's happening in our country and beyond. Our locale, after all, has broadened: high-speed travel, advanced technologies, the Internet, and our cell phones have shrunk our world.

Global village is a familiar phrase; caring global village is not; civil global village is not. Examples come to mind: white supremacists disrupting civil demonstrations in Charlottesville, Virginia; military leaders terrorizing Rohingyas in Myanmar; North Koreans firing ballistic missiles over Japan; and powerful men sexually harassing women in Hollywood—all are part of our global village, and these incivilities are our incivilities. The world is very much with us, to alter William Wordsworth's famous line.[2] Must not our caring sensibility extend to world citizens impacted by cruelties? They are, after all, part of our global village.

A Word on Non-Caring Relationships

As you read through our caring manifesto below, you will likely be measuring your own relationships against the possibilities described herein. You will likely think of some that are less than caring, that are wanting of the caring particulars described here, a real problem if those relationships are intimate ones. Some of the issues that impact caring go to the biases and prejudices you may still hold. It is my hope that our civility practices so far have ameliorated those prejudices, at least to some degree. Yet maybe the "I" you hope for has trouble transforming prejudice to compassion on wish or command. Exhuming the hatred and dislikes of prejudice and bias takes time, self-talk, sometimes decisions to disassociate from those who hate, to leave them behind, to find new associations that enable compassion.

We offer no recipes that guarantee success. Our approach is to develop as positive role models, to create caring as we learn to create civility. Our approach, as demonstrated here, asks that we look at the big picture, set goals that position ourselves within it, and work toward them. A goal here is to show compassion to all in our communities large and small, regardless of age, race, ethnicity, class, and political or religious beliefs. Compassion surely contributes to the moral basis of the philosophy and practice of civility as we are advocating and adopting it here. Can we tolerate discrimination if we are truly compassionate, if we are truly civil? Our first three processes focus inward and so involve self-determination; here we look outward at relationships that connect us to others and so invite uncertainty.

Early on, I asked you to adopt and proclaim the ideal. I realize my words carry a ring of naivete, in that they ask so much of so many, so much that has proved incontrovertible in the past. I acknowledge our days can be difficult when we live with or near racists, for example, or near any of those filled with hateful narrow-mindedness toward the other; or when our leaders absolve themselves of idealism; or when those around us seem resistant to change and to working toward the common good; or when cruel people lash out against the change you are hoping to inspire. You will find that compassion takes the courage that we have seen in those who embrace activism to effect civil change.

A Caring Meditation

As mindfulness helps with the integrative processes we undertake, let us begin with an expansive meditation, a civility shawl settled around our shoulders, and a compassionate concern for ourselves and others, filling our meditative space. Meditation is a gift we give ourselves, a release from the hurriedness, a centering process. Caring for ourselves allows deep caring for others.

> Our process is familiar, deep meditative breathing, this time within the aura of truly caring people, those who have helped reduce our pain or actualize a dream; who have truly shared our reality; who are separate yet with us.
>
> Pause, breathe into a state of compassionate caring. Progressively relax. Move through a body scan, which you are doing in minutes now, in a caring aura.
>
> Sustaining mindfulness, carry out the civility wings yoga practice, arms and hands up, slowly out, then down and around, bringing civility itself unto you. Then again, stretching arms and hands up and around, their circle pushing fairness, awareness, and harmony outward, drawing humanity and caring, in.

In caring, we personify civility. Pause. Repeat. Breathe.

Now focus on your identity reformation, breathing into your gender, race, religion, and politics, acknowledging who you are socially. Recall poignant, significant insights from your identity interrogation. Smiling, breathe into your bodyheartmindsoul as a civility habitat, sensitive to understandings and vulnerabilities realized through our study so far. Pause. Breathe. Resist exclusion, welcome inclusion. Pause. It's a lot to take in. Yet taking it in through our breathing. We are one with our identity transformation. It infuses our fairness, awareness, and harmony.

Always a process, process itself a basis of meditation, process itself bringing us the possibility of civility.

Imagine infusing good vibrations into acts of compassion. Breathe deeply and slowly. Our senses fully aware, absorbing, integrating. Pause. Breathe. Through caring we approach full humanity.

Moving out of meditation but staying in mindful composure, go deep and see if you can evoke your first memories of caring, of being cared for, when you were very much affected by those who held you, by their states of mind and sense of well-being. How comforting those feelings are, if you can evoke them.

Move now to a memory of holding a newborn. You are in a profound relationship—mother or father, relative or friend, holding a new life, connected in pure harmony to an infant as pure humanity. Even though you may not have found words with which to verbalize the sensation, you feel what our Milton Mayeroff calls the "extraordinary, deep-seated intelligibility in life . . . the unfathomable character of existence."[3]

Newborns, with their incipient senses, must feel this too, given their propensity to snuggle and respond to touch. Parents and caregivers sense this amazing, pure state, and reciprocate. Their reciprocation includes love, and more—an awareness of life potential in its purity. All things going well, an acceptance too, a natural readiness to embrace the newborn as they are. A sensuous impulse to care reverberates.

Our early memories, if we could retrieve them, say, through deepest meditation, would be a cooing (aaahhh, dear one, look at you, ooohhh, so precious, so miraculous), and stroking (aaahhh, your skin so soft, satiny, wrinkled, complete) and seeing (smiles in amazement, wrinkled brows wondering, hands covering, and cleaning). Hearing and touching and seeing—all with an impulse to care, to protect, to help along, to make life possible.

Our assumption is that caring itself is an emotional, protective impulse that is distributed equally in men and women, although manifested differently. We recognize that caregiving has traditionally fallen to mothers, following nature's design of breastfeeding. We recognize also the positive value of altering caregiving roles to accommodate changing social roles. Children see this new behavior and adopt it. We recognize the brilliant feminist theorists who examine and redefine possibilities for relationships, and the trove of people who practice their thinking. Caring is fundamental to the interactive process of any people seeking common good.

Caring in Relationships

In the sense in which people can ever be said to be at home in their world, they are at home not through dominating, or explaining, or appreciating, but through caring and being cared for.
—Milton Mayeroff

How do we develop our capacity for caring? Our capacity to help others be at home in the world? How does doing so relate to civility and to the role of citizen we are claiming?

A myriad of approaches present themselves. One could say that the entire field of the humanities devotes itself to relationships, through its examination of the human condition; that anthropology, psychology, and sociology each has its own enlightening take on such relationships, as do political science and history and philosophy.

But here we forego subject-area or discipline-centric approaches and position ourselves in more general understandings.

The work of two humanist scholars—both philosophers who write on care theory—shape our thinking: the aforementioned Milton Mayeroff brings the mind of a psychiatrist to *On Caring,* and Nel Noddings provides an educator's perspective to *Caring: A Feminine Approach to Ethics and Moral Education.* Mayeroff describes a more holistic life anchored in caring. Drawing on her experience as an educator, Noddings goes more to the specific and describes characteristics and behaviors of the-one-caring and the-one-cared for. Working within these frameworks gives a manageable way to talk about the expansive nature of caring and its potential for reimagining civility.

Mayeroff describes the nature and disposition of a life ordered through caring, while Noddings discusses distinctive talents and skills of those in caring relationships. Mayeroff describes qualities, Noddings characteristics. The Commitment to Caring graphic captures the complexities of caring.

Mayeroff and "A Life Ordered through Caring"

If others are to grow through my caring, they must trust me, for only then will they open themselves to me and let me help them.

—Milton Mayeroff

Mayeroff tells us that "a life ordered through caring," has

- an open, accessible, continuing certainty rooted in the world;
- a feeling that the process of life itself is enough, renewed and developed as it is through "exercise";
- intelligibility and unfathomability;
- autonomy;
- faith; and
- gratitude.[4]

These qualities are conceptualized in our graphic as floating in the sky above us. I suggest you take a meditative moment and slowly reread the list above—breathing into each of these qualities, absorbing them into your being. Scan the graphic and imagine caring as described: on an inbreath, suffuse "a life ordered through caring" down to your toes and on a slow outbreath, infuse from your toes through your bodyheartmindsoul "an open, accessible, continuing certainty rooted in the world."

For Mayeroff, caring is a way of life, and here we are folding caring into our practice of civility as a way of life. Regarding gratitude, for example, Mayeroff writes, "I thank life by caring for this or that instance of it."[5] A mindful and beautiful conceptualization. These qualities, taken as a whole, possess a mindful, vibratory, dynamic nature and convey an attitude of openness and generosity. A "life ordered through caring" is one of inclusivity. Mayeroff's list is another way of thinking of full humanity.

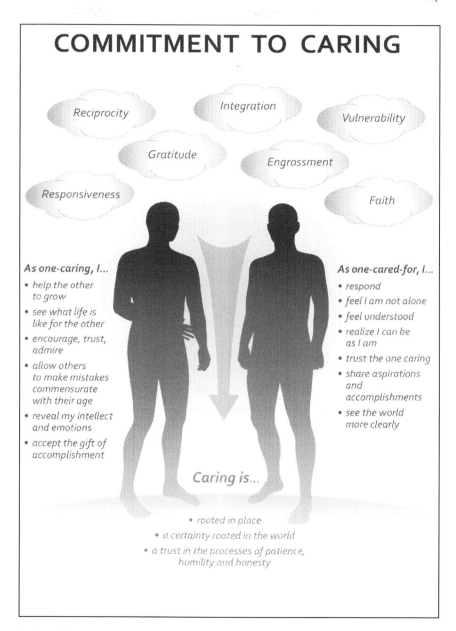

COMMITMENT TO CARING

Reciprocity

Integration

Vulnerability

Gratitude

Engrossment

Responsiveness

Faith

As one-caring, I...

* help the other to grow
* see what life is like for the other
* encourage, trust, admire
* allow others to make mistakes commensurate with their age
* reveal my intellect and emotions
* accept the gift of accomplishment

As one-cared-for, I...

* respond
* feel I am not alone
* feel understood
* realize I can be as I am
* trust the one caring
* share aspirations and accomplishments
* see the world more clearly

Caring is...

* rooted in place
* a certainty rooted in the world
* a trust in the processes of patience, humility and honesty

Adapted from Milton Mayeroff, *On Caring* and Nel Noddings, *Caring. Illustration by Susan Panning.*

For Mayeroff, caring is always *in situ*—it is positioned, or located, in the place where we are. This truth aligns caring as we are defining it with civility, which is also always in situ. Mayeroff says that through caring "something fundamentally new has occurred in our lives, like the change that occurs in our living when we come to take full responsibility for our lives.[6]

Let us explore further how Mayeroff links caring with place. He writes:

> We are 'in-place' in the world through having our lives ordered by inclusive caring. . . . My feeling of being in place is not entirely subjective, and it is not merely a feeling, for it expresses my actual involvements with others in the world. Place is not something I have, as if it were a possession. Rather *I am in-place because of the way I relate to others*. And place must be continually renewed and reaffirmed; it is not assured once and for all, for it is our response to the need of others to grow which gives us place[7] (emphasis mine).

And finally, "[P]lace is not a thing or a fixed state. We may think of ourselves as restless, in some deep-seated sense, until we find our unique place, and of being in-place as coming to rest, but this rest is dynamic rather than static."[8]

The same can be said for civility: through creating civility, in this moment, in this place, something fundamentally new occurs in our lives, such as the change that occurs in our living when we come to take full responsibility for our lives.

We have been heading in this direction all along. Taking full responsibility for our lives is central to our civility transformation. Put another way, when we find civility, we (re)create ourselves.

Let us pause for another meditative moment in order to reread Mayeroff's incisive passages above as a meditation, with measured breathing. I want you to get in the practice of meditating on a moment, one that touches your felt sense, in this case allowing Mayeroff to guide you to a fuller understanding of caring.

Think through Mayeroff's constellation of caring qualities and let them infuse your being, your bodyheartmindsoul. Breathe slowly into each quality, coaxing each into your own caring being. Certainty. Intelligibility.

Autonomy. Faith. Gratitude. Unfathomability, a quality that surpasses our ability to name.

In taking them in, embody the dynamic of caring in order to bring it into you. Our embodied, self-organized mind exists both within and between, giving caring its capaciousness. In this meditative moment, we absorb caring. Feel caring's accessibility as we absorb its qualities, going slowly, breathing into each of them.

Breathe into this idea that links caring and place: "our response to the need of others to grow which gives us place." This idea gives worth to our study—of linking caring to place, where civility blossoms. Deep concentration, resonating to caring, which gives us a place in the world.

Slowly absorb the qualities of caring, thus making their rich and deep sense available, as one might repeat commandments: "Thou shall convey an open, accessible, continuing certainty rooted in the world." And so on.

Imagine our lives anchored in caring, and in the qualities of life as we are learning to embody them. Create civility wings and imagine them bringing caring into your being.

Herein is a lesson for making common cause with the others: people yearn to belong, to be connected to one another. Remember times when you were new to a place and felt you didn't yet fit in—such an awkward, vulnerable feeling. By weaving Mayeroff's wisdom into our bodyheart-mindsouls, and into our meditations and journaling, we create the mood and context necessary for finding common ground, eventually for peace-making.

It is likely that you have been comparing your own experience of caring "in place" to that described by Mayeroff. Recall that in our identity interrogation, we listed place as one of our identity markers. Both who we are and how we learned to care are related to place. I analyze the relationship in the passage below.

All six of my siblings' lives (and mine) have been enriched and haunted by our experience on our farm. Each one of us has a different experience of it, yet our very souls are linked to it in unfathomable ways. In watching growth among ourselves and in our plantings, we learned how to care for something other than ourselves, to nourish it, and still care for ourselves. We left the farm, but it did not leave us.

Did my yearning for a life rooted in civility begin in our garden, in our wheat fields, in our little woods across the road where each spring we looked for jack-in-the-pulpits?

I have moved ten times in my life, three one-year moves, barely time to plant caring in my tiny habitats. The planting metaphor makes clear the challenge of each move. I uprooted myself from who and what I cared for.

Uncle Dave thought moving away from one's place of birth was immoral, a belief he made clear to me whenever I came home. At the time I railed against his assertion. Now I wonder over the implications of leaving what has been planted—certainly an issue that wreaks family havoc in these days of itinerancy. Still, as Tocqueville pointed out so long ago, this spirit of exploration is in the American soul and—perhaps even more fundamentally—in the human soul, as we are coming to understand the itinerancy of our primate and prehistoric ancestors.

Now turn to your journal and write about how your own sense of caring is linked to place. Recall that Mayeroff says we are "in-place" because of the way we relate to others. Recount an experience in which your sense of being "in-place" came about through caring for another, in a particular place. Can you figure out the nuanced relationship between caring, "in-place" and place? That is, of how caring made you feel in-place within a certain location, of how your fondness for or attachment to a place goes to the care you gave or received there? As I write, I think of the oft-repeated "there's no place like home." Mayeroff's analysis shows why that statement rings true: the care you receive there abides, as does a sense of place. As I write, I realize I must acknowledge the negative, that not all places are marked by caring, that it is possible to be *in* a place and never feel "in-place" because of caring's absence. That too is worth remarking on in your journal.

You can turn to any one of those qualities Mayeroff connects to caring—certainty, intelligibility, autonomy, faith, and gratitude—and tease out how they are involved in the caring experiences you have

known. Notice and comment on their expansive connotation; they all help you to be more than you now are, as caring itself does, as the empathy that we are striving for does. Perhaps the most intriguing quality Mayeroff names is that of unfathomability. Have you been fortunate enough to either give or receive care when that experience was simply impossible to measure the extent of or to describe? Unpacking such an experience will be a way to inscribe caring in your soul.

Nel Noddings and "[M]eet[ing] the Other in Caring"

Everything depends . . . upon the will to be good, to remain in caring relation to the other. How may we help ourselves and each other to attain this will?

[O]ne must meet the other in caring. From this there is no escape for one who would be moral.

—Nel Noddings

I take the "meet[ing] other in caring" phrase from *Caring*'s final sentences. I would add that if we are to meet the other in civility, there is no escape from caring.

My reading of Noddings tells me she would embrace Mayeroff's thinking; indeed, she lists him in her bibliography. But her focus differs. She describes caring as a feminine approach to ethics and moral education. She goes to some length to explain her use of the feminine, an explanation important enough to include in the note below, as the issue is still with us today.[9]

Noddings is an educator as well as a philosopher. For her, caring is all about action, doing, and relationships. Mayeroff, our psychiatrist, is more about the mind and our state of being, the action subsumed in his conceptualization—a lovely and useful complementarity.

I invite you to measure your own experience of caring against the particulars below, reading mindfully, to integrate caring into your bodyheartmindsoul. When have you, in your caring experiences, already internalized what Noddings is describing? The very process of definition increases our capacity for knowing. When we get it, we can embody it.

Noddings focuses on caring in relationships—the nature of the relationship itself and the roles of both the one-caring and the one-cared-for. Both parties will be responsive to one another, responsive in that they are engrossed in the relationship. Hence, they will be vulnerable to the exchanges that occur as the relationship develops—its emotionality, intellectuality, and intimacy. There will be sharing, and that sharing (say, of goals and aspirations) brings the mutual dependence of reciprocity. Finally, if the caring relationship is to continue and to thrive, both the one-caring and the one-cared-for must integrate what is developing in the relationship. Noddings means these qualities to be true of all caring relationships. Her very naming of the roles expresses her concern for the necessity of caring in teacher-student relationships.

Noddings tells us that, as the ones-caring, we "receive the other onto us"; we feel with him or her. We reveal our intellectual and emotional powers. We share why we are in the game and our doing so reveals our authenticity. When caring clicks, we are buoyed by the response. We acknowledge the exchange and name its gift, whether an insight or something else to wonder over. Noddings explains:

> I set aside my temptation to analyze and to plan. I do not project; *I receive the other into myself*, and I see and feel with the other. . . . My rational powers are not diminished but they are enrolled in the service of my engrossment in the other.[10] (emphasis mine)

In our engrossment, we are receptive, admittedly vulnerable, "totally with the other, . . . allowing [our] motive energy to be shared. . . . putting it at the service of the other."[11]

Let us pause for reflection. As the one-caring, have you not embodied these characteristics? The first four—feeling, receiving, revealing, sharing—show your responsiveness and engrossment and surely leave you vulnerable. The buoyancy of the response, the reciprocity, and the culmination all lead to wonder.

Our questors after the ideal—you, me, members of your civility circle, along with those stalwarts of civility we learned of back in the day or witnessed in our own day—all possess these capacities of someone who cares. We see them revealed in great writers' stories, past and present, fiction and nonfiction, and in poetry too. We hear them treasured through storytelling. Think of the staying power of *StoryCorps* on National Public Radio. We also know them through our own deep relationships. In civility, we care for those who are different from us. Our caring is inclusive. We do not take comfort in a neutral position, as I did to the black women who lived next to me in my college dormitory. I must acknowledge that my behavior was racist. We learn to reach out in caring ways. Such is the morality at the heart of civility. Such is the action at the heart of caring.

Noddings makes clear that caring is a two-way street. The ones-cared-for also have responsibilities. They receive the care, acknowledge the care, and respond, thus evincing engrossment. They share aspirations, apprais-als, and accomplishments. Thus, the reciprocity is set in motion, the reception becoming part of what the one-caring feels. In the teacher-student relationship, students do not have to receive the teacher (the one-caring) as the teacher receives them. Yet the teacher must respond somehow. *"There is, necessarily, a form of reciprocity in caring"* (emphasis mine).[12] This necessity for reciprocity is true of all caring relationships.

In other words, the behavior of one-caring is completed in the one-cared-for. As Noddings points out, this truth is consistent with observations of the philosopher Martin Buber, who says of the reciprocity of a relationship: "One should not try to dilute the meaning of the relation: relation is reciprocity."[13] Noddings confirms: "What the cared-for gives to the relation either in direct response to the one-caring or in personal delight or in happy growth before her eyes is genuine reciprocity."[14]

While there is admittedly a status difference between the one-caring and the cared-for in our example above, status differences, and even gender roles, generally fold into the engrossment that emerges in the reciprocity, with the status differences dissipating. It takes time for the engrossment of caring reciprocity to become a habit, and so it is important to continue listening and standing under the particulars of difference, as we learned in Accountability Listening in Process #3.

Let us imagine a discussion of difference, say, by two people, or two groups of people, representing community groups of differing opinions and agendas but finding common cause in a kind of reciprocal give-and-take. Eventually, in discussions among those of more or less equal status, the one-caring and cared-for roles change, or fade into the background; the engrossment, receptivity, and reciprocity that characterize the caring relationship move to the foreground. Roles switch.

We are restored in civility in the exchange. The engrossment of recep-tivity and reciprocity comes naturally too. We feel our engrossment as integrative, as a process that opens possibilities.

We are open to the vulnerability that caring brings. Drawing on memories of caring in infancy and of precious caring moments, we integrate civility—and the caring that comes along with it—into our lives. Caring will serve us well, in our effort to become Earth citizens. We will help our world as it heads toward integration.

Caring Flow

It is useful to consider an array of caring relationships—all with a potential for civility, the array involving different levels of gravitas, yet all having stakes in serving humanity. I suggest below a range of potential relationships. These represent a continuum of caring possibility, a lesser to greater commitment. Our caring is anchored in civility; we "meet 'the other' in caring."

The array shows people and principles merging, the more complete associations carrying an idea of earlier ones. It is possible to jump into the middle of any one of them. It is worth remembering that relationships proceed from the memory of having been cared for. I suggest an array below:

- detachment (yet cradling potential caring and goodness);
- association (initial steps to civility that run through deeper associations; ethical behavior permeates);
- affiliation (next steps)
- empathic relatedness (a capacity to experience and share emotional moments);
- compassionate relatedness (assumes empathy, sympathetic pity, and concern, especially for misfortune and suffering); and
- consubstantial relatedness (substantially with, full identification, oneness).

I conclude with a word suited for our purposes—*consubstantiality*. The rhetorician Kenneth Burke seeks consubstantiality when the speaker, audience, and speech are necessarily separate, so often the case when incivilities occur in groups and when there is little if any agreement. For Burke, consubstantiality occurs when one is moved to remake the substance of his or her identity into a state of oneness with the other. Our processes also work toward this end.

Burke looks for an "overlapping"[15] of ideas so that the two parties eventually become substantially with one another. The concept offers promise as an ultimate goal for coming together, given incivilities that are rife across the world. Indeed, Burke was writing after the tragedies of WWII.

Another scholar, our contemporary Daniel Shea, in "Our Tribal Nature and the Rise of Nasty Politics," describes something like Burke's consubstantiation:

> [T]here is our sense of empathy—that uniquely human characteristic that allows individuals to relate, care, and connect. Beyond our politics, religion, values, sexual orientation, race, and all our other differences, our capacity to care remains.[16]

Toward Communities (and Countries) of Civility

Our capacity to care is shown in the huge amount of volunteerism that supports numerous causes in our communities, small and large—individual and organizational good deeds that promote health and wellbeing. Our volunteerism anchors us to a place—our communities, real and virtual—and provides us benefits amounting to happiness, enriching our lives by caring for those beyond our family circle, and understanding some of the issues communities face in the process. It is not a stretch to say that volunteerism makes us better citizens: we see and feel for a community and its challenges in new ways.

Individuals, and indeed organizations, have little trouble finding significant and personally meaningful ways to extend caring to others. But how do cities themselves become caring? How can they transform themselves into cities of civility? How do countries do the same?

Creating a New Civility offers ways for communities to wrestle with civility as they discuss economic and social realities. Imagine communities undertaking an identity exploration as a point of departure for their actions.

As I write this segment, I am reading Ta-Nehisi Coates's *We Were Eight Years in Power: An American Tragedy*. I read short sections at a time, my conscience struck anew by my country's plunder of black people. The incivilities are haunting.

In the chapter on "The Case for Reparations," I notice the section on the realtor's code of ethics that was in force as late as 1950, which stated that a "realtor should never be instrumental in introducing into a neighborhood . . . any race or nationality, or any individuals whose presence will clearly be detrimental to property values."[17]

The passage hits home. When as a little girl I wondered why no black people lived in Shelby, mother speculated that real estate agents and land value played roles in keeping them out. Yet the excuse was, "They wouldn't be happy here." Not the truth: we were keeping them out. We were not welcoming them, not inviting them in. Case in point: as a little girl, I remember a new Methodist minister came to town whose wife needed full-time health care; her black caregiver was not allowed to live in the parsonage and had to take the bus daily from nearby Mansfield.

Where was our civility? Few of us understood the concept of white privilege then and most still don't. Many still inhabit this incivility and don't understand how it diminishes their full humanity. Mother gave me a glimmer of understanding, which led me to make a pitch for reparations and repair.

HR. 40 and S.1083 call for the study and development of reparation proposals for the descendants of slaves. In mentioning these bills, I strive to make a point about our country's capacity to care, and how that capacity advances our sense of civility. I believe that offering reparations to descendants of slaves says loud and clear that we care. Ta-Nehisi Coates, with whom we began our identity exploration, testified in a congressional hearing on behalf of HR.40, arguing that "we are American citizens, and thus bound to a collective enterprise that extends beyond our individual and personal reach." Slavery and its immense consequences, he explains, are part of that enterprise. "In HR.40," he asserts, "[Congress] has a chance to both make good on its 2009 apology for enslavement, and reject fair-weather patriotism, to say that this nation is both its credits and debits. That if Thomas Jefferson matters, so does Sally Hemings. . . ."[18]

Coates develops a similar theme in *We Were Eight Years in Power*. He writes:

> I believe that wrestling publicly with these questions matters as much
> as—if not more than—the specific answers that might be produced. An
> America that asks what it owes its most vulnerable citizens is improved

and humane. An America that looks away is ignoring not just the sins of the past but the sins of the present and the certain sins of the future. More important than any single check cut to any African American, the payment of reparations would represent America's maturation out of the childhood myth of its innocence into a wisdom worthy of its founders.[19]

Our interest in reparation and repair arises out of caring for the people on whose backs our country has been built and who face continuing injustices, many of which derive from a past impoverished in so many ways. Our communities need to ask themselves, "Who are we?" as we did in our identity interrogation when we examined our own racial provenance. So, our thinking ends up being valuable not only for our personal lives but also for the public lives of our communities and our country.

Coming full circle, Mayeroff reminds us that, in caring, "[s]omething fundamentally new [occurs] in our lives, like the change that occurs in one's life when one comes to take full responsibility for it."[20] The change from caring is as dramatic as the change that comes when we take full responsibility for our lives. By engaging in civility, we are taking full responsibility for our lives. I am buoyed by the possibilities of creating a new civility, in gratitude for the very rich sense of civility understanding we are gaining in pleating our processes together, adding the complexity and capaciousness of caring to our quest. As you create civility, I hope that you experience moments of high drama and wonder. They will be comparable to taking responsibility for your life. Our founding fathers believed that. So did Emerson, Thoreau, Rosa Parks, and Martin Luther King. You are following in their tradition.

Before you turn to the section on reasoning well, take time to weave together the strands of your thinking on civility. Perhaps you want to turn to the introduction and review your civility pledge, as you are committed to the practice of civility, aware that your understanding of civility is growing in theory and in practice. Are you keeping your civility journal close at hand in order to record insights worthy of remembering, perhaps sharing, and certainly to build on? When you find a moment, are you sitting in mindful meditation, breathing into the wonders of the day, the frustrations and challenges—and into an abiding sense of civility itself as a way to express your humanity? In doing so, you are caring for yourself.

A Collocation of Caring Qualities

According to the *Oxford Dictionary*, linguists use collocation to mean a "juxtaposition or association of a particular word with other particular words; a group of words so associated."

I am fond of lists and definitions, as you know by now, and the insights they make possible, so I list a collocation of caring qualities below, alphabetically, suggesting that you, dear reader, using the worksheet that follows, arrange the characteristics so that they move from a modicum of caring qualities to completely absorbed or consubstantial caring, from initial to complete commitment. Try to show the emerging complexity of caring relationships. Notice the list begins with "Initial Commitment" and concludes with "Consubstantiality" (the sense of being, recall, that Kenneth Burke describes as overlapping, or substantially with). Compare and contrast your completed lists with members of your civility circle. Parents, if this activity is age-appropriate, have your children arrange the list and explain their arrangement to you.

In making distinctions, you come to understand what I am fondly referring to as the capaciousness of caring, from initial commitment to the emotional heft of Burke's being-with, of consubstantiality.

On one hand, reflection leads me to think, "No wonder these fully caring and civil relationships are so hard to achieve." On the other I think, "Not so hard. We have realized them through fairness, awareness, harmony, and now in caring." I am not suggesting an idea of caring flow or a strict process of development. That is for you to do. It isn't cheating to consult a dictionary to confirm your understanding of a word. There is room for give and take. Give yourselves over to the flow, which allows the hesitation, regression, accommodation, and energy renewal that occurs in thinking through a cause and committing to it. Always a process, caring flow, folding caring into civility. I invite you to add more examples of your own that you believe are critical to caring. It'll be fun to discuss the logic of your arrangements with others who care about caring and civility.

A Collocation of Caring Qualities

Using your own experience of caring, arrange the qualities below to culminate in consubstantiation.

Joy's List, Alphabetized

Initial Commitment

Ability to Relate

Bodily Involvement

Comfort

Confirmation

Emotionality

Engrossment

Familiarity

Harmony

Identification

Kindness

Lessening Restraint

Mercy

Receptivity

Reciprocity

Relationship reverberation

Respect

Responsiveness

Reader's List of Caring Flow

Initial Commitment

_____

_____

_____

_____

_____

_____

_____

_____

_____

_____

_____

_____

_____

_____

_____

_____

_____

Social cohesion   _____

Tolerance   _____

Willingness to listen   _____

Consubstantiation   Consubstantiation

(substantially with another, in substance, overlapping)

Memory Work
Caring with Milton Mayeroff and Nel Noddings in Journaling and Civility Circles

As you answer the questions below, you can also meditate on each of them, following deep breathing guidelines as you focus and proceed. The meditative mindset allows you to recall the felt sense of these situations, allowing for insight.

Define some ways in which civility is coming to life within and around you.

> Recall and write about a time when, through caring, you felt *in situ*, "in place," because of the way you related to others. Recall that Mayeroff would say that being in place "expresses your actual involvements with others in the world."
>
> Has something "fundamentally new" come into your life through caring? How so?
>
> Recalling Mayeroff's definition, remember a time when you were in "the full state of caring": being rooted in the world, feeling life as if it were enough, with its intelligibility and unfathomability, autonomy, faith, and gratitude.
>
> Remember another time when caring involved any of what Noddings says it does: responsiveness, reciprocity, engrossment, vulnerability, and integration.
>
> Remember another time when being cared for evinced, as Noddings says, engrossment, and resulted in a sharing of aspirations, appraisals, and accomplishments:
>
> Study a significant "interdependent" group relationship from the point of view of the caring consciousness-raising we learned in Exploration #4. See yourself in the larger social fabric of the group. How are you, and other group members, working to make common cause with the other? How has civility underpinned or floated as a theme throughout the relationship? If not, why not? Given the civility strategies that you are accumulating, what remedies might allow civility to serve as a pivotal point around which the relationship might grow?

Looking back over your responses to Processes #1, #2, and #3, what themes emerge that impede your ability to care?

How have your bodyheartmindsoul meditations opened possibilities for caring?

What possibilities for caring have opened up through our listening lessons, particularly those emerging from our four kinds of active listening: say back, contemplative, compassionate, and accountability?

Process #5
Reasoning Well—
Toward Insight

There is no such thing as a neutral education process. Education either functions as an instru-ment which is used to facilitate the integration of generations into the logic of the present system and bring about conformity to it, or it becomes the "practice of freedom," the means by which men and women deal critically with reality and discover how to participate in the transformation of their world.
—Richard Shaull

Brazilian educator Paulo Freire would say that, through our explora-tions, we have been taking responsibility for "making and remaking our-selves," in our case, as beings capable of civility. We, as civility change agents, are participating in the transformation of our world.

To do that, we must reason well. We have reasoned our way through these processes, implicitly so. Here we find an explicit way to reason well, our culminating process in the creation of civility, undertaken in the name of justice.

There are no easy exercises to shape us up for civility, and, indeed, our processes so far have involved considerable complexity, manageable yet rewarding enough that they are imbued in our being so that we can practice them in our lives.

What magic might we find to help us with this culminating process of reasoning well? What demonstration that will untangle the threads in the dynamics of civility, as that of a magician untangling fingers, shirt cuffs and collars, appendages, and prompts—feathers, scarfs, hats, cards, coins, and so forth—in the magic act. But there must be no sleight of hand. So where do we turn? To that which has (almost) always been: rhetoric, as the rational way humans from classical times, from East and West, have shaped content, and therefore meaning, in their lives.

I offer two "short courses" that get to basics, assured that our rhetorical heritage will serve our civility intentions. This rhetorical turn reminds us how long humans have been interested in the positive transformation of their world. As we extend our civility practice to the interdependence of us all in our world today, we draw on good thinking across time and place as well.

Rhetoric has the tools to help us understand communication dynamics. In the bargain, we will gain insights on moral grounding and ethical accountability. Its tools bring specificity to analysis. We don't have to look at a situation, make a guess, analyze on the basis of a generalization, decide on the basis of hearsay or what has been done before, and grope our way to a decision. With rhetoric, we can reason well.

Our first short course deals with situational context, and the second with acts and their motives, also as they occur in context. These models are complex and the tools within them are not magic. With the help of two practice rounds, we will be able to read contentious situations and incivil acts, and to think on our feet in order to analyze and shape ongoing discussions. We won't be able to do such analysis instantly, but practice will help us integrate the reasoning. These frameworks then become part of our developing civility intelligence. They are tools to get at trust as well as truth. In each model, we look at the parameters and think them through to get to a good decision, one we can be accountable for, one that has been articulated before we mark our ballots, for example.

Our first four processes have helped us prepare for this last stop on our journey, where we hone our skills at reasoning on behalf of the greater good. Indeed, reasoning well builds on the very foundations of fairness, awareness, harmony, and compassion. The models help us frame the context of any situation, which, in turn, helps our reasoning to be sound,

accountable, and nondivisive. Our aim is truth-telling in the name of
democracy.

Remember: no quick fixes, no thirty-day program. We look explicitly
at the world of reason, realizing we have been reasoning all along, although
implicitly rather than explicitly as here in our final process. Here we go.
Our quest is at its culminating moment: we are about to realize fully the
creation of civility in preparation for maintaining our democracy.

Reasoning and the Practice of Freedom

My goal for you in this fifth process is twofold: to give you practice analyzing situations to see if and how civility emerges, and, ultimately, to put
your knowledge to work as a civility advocate or activist. We are developing
our civility *gravitas*, the seriousness with which we take our individual contributions to common cause in order to shape the destiny of civility.

To get at the dynamics of civility, we will review how meaning gets
made in a situation—by the players in it, the subject at hand, the context,
the action involved, and so on.

I would not attempt to deal with such complexity if I did not have in
mind some brilliant thinkers who can help us along. Nor would I attempt
to address such complexity without two frameworks that lay out communication dynamics in a memorable way—frameworks that are summarized
in elegant graphic form to help you along in your understanding. It will
be up to you to sort out the (in)civilities within and among the dynamics.

It would be wise for me to give you a flavor of what rhetoric and rhetoricians do before we turn to our models. "The study and practice of
shaping content," is the simplest good definition I know of the complex
field of rhetoric.[1]

Kenneth Burke, familiar to us from the culmination of our caring
process (recall consubstantiation as the culmination of caring in Process
#4), describes rhetoric as "the use of language to shape attitudes and influ-
ence action."

He writes (the italics are his):

> [R]hetoric . . . is rooted in an essential function of language itself, a function that is wholly
> realistic, and is continually born anew: [it is] the use of language as a symbolic means of
> inducing cooperation in beings that by nature respond to symbols.[2]

Richard Weaver calls rhetoric "the most humanistic of the humanities."[3]

As you can see, rhetoric's scope is broad, and, as such, inherently suited for civility. We draw here on fundamental principles of meaning-making that have stood the test of time and translate them to civility practice. The process is apropos, as in meaning-making for civility, we are simultaneously realizing our human potential and inducing cooperation in a humanistic way.

I must add that meaning-making principles of Eastern philosophers are generally expressed more introspectively than those reviewed above; their philosophic thought also goes to the idea of compassionate living for the common good, in the examples of Confucius, of Buddha, and more recently, of the Dalai Lama. Their ideas help us understand what it means to live a civil life. Their philosophy underpins mindful awareness and is relevant in listening, caring, and here, in reason, especially as it gets at the balance of all things.

As we proceed, I ask you to dismiss your association to "It's all just rhetoric!"

As you will see, the "just rhetoric" phrase is dangerous, and often rides on an incivility itself. Blowing off the high-flown, blustery speeches of a politician as "just rhetoric" disregards centuries of serious thought about how language works in written and spoken form. Not knowing about the study and practice of shaping content limits understanding, as well as the full realization of human potential. Even though language is not always used to manipulate, knowing when it is used that way helps us understand the dynamics at play (for example, when the government faces shutdown over the inability of our president and congressional legislators to reach agreement, or when legislators place party loyalty over common good).

Before we turn to the philosopher/rhetoricians who will inform our thinking, let us explore the rhetorical abilities we naturally bring to a situation, whether we have formalized rhetorical knowledge or not.

Most of us are pretty good at sizing up a situation. Whether conscious of it or not, we scan who is present, what they are talking about, the feeling we get from the resonance in the room, how we might fit in and catch up to speed in the conversation, and possibly contribute. "What happened when Auntie went for her interview?" or "You're saying Josh got notice of downsizing?" or "What's that new ring on your left hand?" or "Oh my, they're working over the relationship between Donald Trump and Vladimir Putin again!"

These discussions concern those we love, work, play, volunteer with, and perhaps go to church with. We size up situations well when the scene and the people are familiar, when we are with family and friends. We know their various belief systems and histories. We know something of the context of their lives. The conversation moves along, meaning gets made, and understanding emerges. Assuming we don't want to antagonize or tease, we know how to build a civil situation.

In this fifth and final exploration, we are looking at how meaning gets made and how content is shaped in less familiar situations that involve others. We think seriously about all that comes naturally when we are with family and friends. All we have learned is brought to the fore: being with ourselves and others in our identity scan, in mindful awareness, in the good vibrations of the space around us, and in caring flow.

Your workplace likely comes to mind as a rich source for analyzing civility dynamics. Your church services and their related activities are another. So are meetings of social groups such as book clubs, of civic groups such as parent-teacher, town hall, community governance associations, and online communities. You will be able to apply what you learn to the national scene too, and to moments you see play out on television, such as presidential pressers, for example, newscasts, and congressional meetings, foremost of which is the State of the Union address.

I still remember Joe Wilson's egregious "You lie!" scream during President Obama's address to a joint session of Congress, although it occurred a decade ago. Perhaps President Trump's most frequent incivility is name-calling that approaches disparagement and vulgarity, as in Crooked Hillary and Sleepy Creepy Joe, "shithole" countries, Mexican immigrants as criminals and "rapists," a woman who has challenged his sexual conduct as "horseface." The fact that I have so little trouble coming up with examples speaks to the moral decay in the White House. No wonder so many people have asked me to send a copy of my book to President Trump when it is published. Rhetorical situations underpin all momentous public occasions—for example, when Anita Hill challenged Clarence Thomas's fitness for court on the basis of his sexual harassment of her. It is interesting how our understandings of such pivotal situations change: at the time her integrity came into question; we now see these hearings as an early public example of one woman's bravery. The hearing came to the fore as Joe Biden, who is a candidate for the presidency in 2020, sat as a panelist on those hearings. His performance then is being scrutinized now. Have any of the panelists apologized for the way Anita Hill herself was victimized in those hearings? More recently, we had Christine Blasey Ford's questioning of Brett Kavanaugh's fitness for the Supreme Court to analyze rhetorically, with its own set of problematic exchanges.

Reasoning, with a Focus on Situation

The Dynamics of Situations graphic is a good representation of the totality of any situation. Review it before we proceed and mark it for future reference. Part of its value is that it gives you a vocabulary in which to frame your analysis. Participants in my presentations have found this graphic, as well as the one that follows, extremely useful in helping them reason well. Why not post them on your refrigerator as a way of bringing everyone into discussions of family dynamics, for example, thus providing a lesson in reasoning?

The relationships laid out in our graphic—among speaker, audience, subject, context, and constraints—have been examined continuously throughout the history of spoken and written communication. Rhetoricians are interested in what gives content its moral basis, so we fold that concern into our discussion as well.

We turn first to the Western, classical thinking of Aristotle, who described rhetoric as "the faculty of observing in any given case the available means of persuasion."[4] Aristotle's means of observation can be conceptualized as an ethos-logos-pathos triangle.

In explaining the interrelationships among ethos, logos and pathos, Aristotle summons a person's resources for effective persuasion. His *Rhetoric* is an attempt to help "in understanding situations in which true knowledge is not available."[5] So often truth in civility dynamics is not always clear, so I am comfortable turning to the ethos-logos-pathos triad as a basis for interpreting situational dynamics. The triad goes to "the whole person, not just to the 'rational being' alone."[6]

As you examine the graphic, you are likely associating ethos with ethics, logos with logic, and pathos with empathy. If so, you are not far

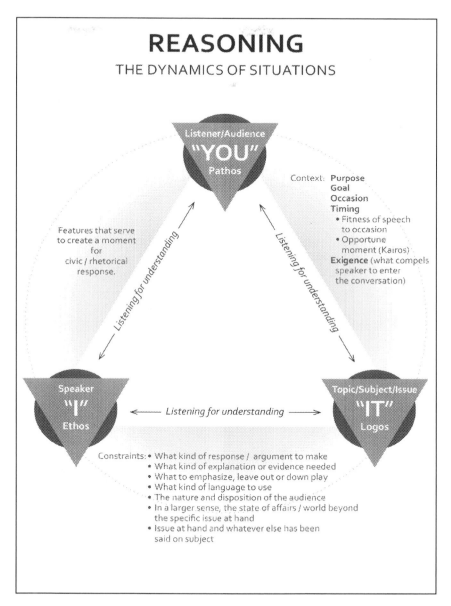

REASONING

THE DYNAMICS OF SITUATIONS

Listener/Audience

"YOU"

Pathos

Context: **Purpose**
Goal
Occasion
Timing
  • Fitness of speech
    to occasion
  • Opportune
    moment (Kairos)
Exigence (what compels
    speaker to enter
    the conversation)

Features that serve
to create a moment
for
civic / rhetorical
response.

Listening for understanding

Listening for understanding

Speaker

"I"

Ethos

⟵——— *Listening for understanding* ———⟶

Topic/Subject/Issue

"IT"

Logos

Constraints: • What kind of response / argument to make
  • What kind of explanation or evidence needed
  • What to emphasize, leave out or down play
  • What kind of language to use
  • The nature and disposition of the audience
  • In a larger sense, the state of affairs / world beyond
    the specific issue at hand
  • Issue at hand and whatever else has been
    said on subject

Diagram adapted from Lloyed F. Bitzer, "The Rhetorical Situation." *Philosophy and Rhetoric. Illustration by Susan Panning.*

afield in understanding what Aristotle had in mind. These three concepts interrelate. Looking at the ethos-logos-pathos dimensions of any situation is a good way to begin unraveling its intricacies.

According to Aristotle, *ethos* is the credibility that each of us carries with us and that we draw on in persuasive arguments. It is based on our good sense or practical wisdom, our moral character, and our good will toward our audience. Our ethos thus projects something of our character as it has been established in our lives so far. In *Creating a New Civility*, we are shaping our ethos. Our identity interrogation goes to our inner substance, our character; perhaps this is where ethos is born or created, and where the bodyheartmindsoul of mindful awareness develops. Our character emerges and radiates as our senses go about their work, especially through listening. Caring consciousness-raising goes to how our character is manifested in the human situation.

Aristotle defines *logos* as a chain of reasoning. Critical to the chain of reasoning is the truth of the premises and facts that play into the reasoning. It is the chain of reasoning that is our primary focus, although we must remember that these three concepts are always already interacting; in that sense, we have been working on all three of them all along. Here we make them explicit.

Pathos goes to the interplay of emotions within the states of mind of the speaker and the audience. Pathos can be equated with empathy, with the emotional relationship between a speaker and the audience and their meaning-making, with the ability of a speaker to understand, even experience vicariously what another is feeling. Ultimately, pathos, as projected through persona and interactions, affects believability and credibility. It is so pleasant to be around someone who can empathize.

Altogether, these three concepts—ethos, logos, and pathos—interact dynamically as a situation evolves and as meaning get made, and changes in the dynamic interplay of an evolving situation. It is as if the three concepts seep into one another, creating the dynamism—a whole person who is attempting to persuade or explain to the listener, another whole person who is making sense; in the process, the meaning evolves as both speaker and listener make sense of the ongoing reasoning. Importantly, the dynamism brings with it a moral tone; it assumes action, based on character, as represented in qualities.

Communication specialists—for example, your former speech or writing teacher—may have presented the triangle as speaker-audience-subject, associating ethos to speaker, pathos to audience, and logos to the subject, topic, or issue under consideration. This common alteration sacrifices nuance yet gets to basic interplay of the triad.

We cannot leave these definitions, though, without noting the issues feminists have with the term *logos*, in that, through its historical construction, it has been a term of exclusion, given that women were considered as less capable by men in reasoning. We must also note Jacques Derrida's deconstructionist belief that, rather than reasoning itself providing truth, as Aristotle would argue, it is language itself that makes possible consciousness and reality. Feminists and deconstructionists would have us add that the very meaning of discourse is contingent on the beliefs and presuppositions that inform the audience's state of mind. Our approach here in *Creating a New Civility* addresses their concerns. The beliefs we hold and how we got to them, as well as how we embody them, are at the very center of our civility study.

Finally, I bring contemporary educator/rhetorician/philosopher James Moffett's modification to the triad. He called the ethos/pathos/logos relationship an I-to-you-about-it relationship, a modification my students find useful, in that it makes the situation less abstract.[7]

Let us analyze the framework in slow motion, graphic at hand, remembering that above all, we wish for reason to prevail in contentious situations in order to get to insight, and knowing that this graphic shows us the components of reason, and something of how they operate, in any situation.

I (speaker) embodying ethos, talk to my audience (you), each of us relating empathically, with pathos, about it (our subject at hand), using logos, a logical chain of reasoning.

Stated another way in order for you to integrate the concept fully:

Speaker (I, ethos) speaks
      to audience (you, listening, pathos "emanating" between us)
         about subject (it, logos, reasoning).

Easy enough. These are basic elements of the rhetorical situation. Every effort to persuade works according to these dynamics. When you as listener take the floor, roles reverse. Most often, speaker and audience are simultaneously present, and the conversation is interactive.

But there is more. To have a meaningful yet civil conversation over how, say, for example, your boss shapes civility in your workplace, we will also have to know something about contexts and constraints that operate in your situation. We don't speak or write in a vacuum, as you'll see below.

The Rhetorical Situation of Creating a New Civility

To help us get a handle on the interactions described above, let us analyze the dynamics of our model. We will use the very example of you reading this book to help us understand them. Think of this as a dry run in getting to the dynamic interplay of speaker/audience/topic/context/constraints in any given situation.

Here goes. Again, keep the graphic at hand. I will try to imagine something of the dynamics that may well be occurring between me as writer and you as reader.

To begin I must answer "Why?" What brought this rhetorical situation into being? I have already answered this pivotal question in my introduction. I want to help people create civility, ultimately for the common good. Your analysis of any situation is an effort after understanding why it came into existence.

In this case, I am a writer talking to you, a reader, a situation in which I have power—I hold the floor and have the evidence of written text (my it), in this case an entire book in which I am making my case about how to create civility.

On the other hand, you as reader have power too. I imagine you frequently talk back to me. You can end the conversation any time by closing the book. In either case, "it" will have to be sustained if civility as we are constructing it is ever to be accomplished.

Let us examine our I/you relationship further, moving into context.

I (writer) know something about you (my audience). If you have stayed with me this long, you are likely committing to a broad sense of civility as I am shaping it, using Adam McClellan's definition as a starting point. I deduce something of your perspective, a bit about your stature as citizen. You and I have something in common, a critical point in establishing a basis for common ground. You are likely to commit to an "interdependence of us all" approach to relationships with others. Our I/you relationship is on the road to full humanity, especially because our shared concerns are so critical. If our concerns were trivial, our relationship would likely be also.

You have ventured into the five processes I have taken up (my it), and are integrating them into your own sense of self. I know you are literate, and beyond that, intelligent enough to have followed my logos throughout our five processes. You are interested in learning. You care for our country. You have the means, whatever they may be, to have discovered this book (my it) however that may have been. Reading my book is part of your own emerging logos, your own effort to create civility. There will have to be a critical mass of people with a similar persona in order for civility as I am describing it here to thrive.

I deduce that you are brave in your willingness to interrogate your identity, having ventured this far and having met me halfway by entertaining my ideas; introspective enough to venture into mindful exploration of your being; sensitive enough to be in touch with the immediacy of your surroundings; engrossed enough to think through the particulars of caring; daring enough to entertain the complexities of civility; and socially and politically conscious enough to act on your beliefs.

Conversely, you know more about me (I) than I know of you. Knowing my concerns for the citizenry and a moral center of civility, you can deduce that I followed the last election closely and am informed about the issues, at least as I see them relating to the civic good (our it). You know something about my background and can guess how it has shaped and is shaping my politics. You have likely come to understand, perhaps come to terms with, my liberal, feminist posture. You know my voice and my concerns. You know something of my way of being in the world. You know something of why I speak, and even of my timing, of why I speak now, my years giving me the wisdom of experience to draw on.

We are understanding something of our particular I/you relationship.

There is less dynamism in our reader-writer (you/I) relationship. You may be talking back to me without my knowing it. I can only intuit what that conversation may be. You may well go out on social media, which we could chart on our graphic as well. You may be sharing my book with another, writing about it in a journal, or talking about it in a civility circle, perhaps advancing my own thinking as you do so. This is how ideas emerge and knowledge develops.

Now let us turn to it, the subject, civility itself. I hope that you are meeting me on my terms (our subject) and absorbing something of them.

Again, we make deductions, given what we know of each other. In this case, I know much less about your interest in civility than you know about mine. If we were to have a real-time conversation over what to make of our subject, my speaker/ethos/character and your listener/pathos/empathic interactions would be teased out as our conversation, it/subject at hand/ logos/line of reasoning makes progress and gains structure. Ah, the complexities!

As author, I hold the floor. If you and I were somehow able to talk together about the book, the conversation and the situation would gain dynamism, with you, me (I), and possibly others switching roles, the subject at hand inevitably complicated. The dynamics revolve around the complexity of each point of the triangle and their interactivity. Our it (subject) is broad, and in the course of our conversation, the situation changes and our very conversation becomes the it. We will be reshaping it as our conversation structures itself around emerging ideas.

Now let's think of how context is operating in our book. The questions below are taken from Lloyd F. Bitzer's "The Rhetorical Situation."[8] Here are the questions we ask: What do I as speaker/writer bring to the conversation? To whom am I speaking? In what situation(s)? What is my purpose? My goal? What is the nature of the occasion? Why does the situation come up at this particular time? What compels me to enter the conversation?

I explicate my text in the next few paragraphs. The context here is narrow in the sense that we examine it within a particular rhetorical situation of your reading of my book. It is larger when we examine it in the ongoing conversation of how civility operates in our world—what we say about it, how and why we say it, and how my book adds to the conversation.

My introduction is largely devoted to context, where I answer the questions listed above. It presents our text as a way to advance civility by helping readers understand what civility is and how to embody it. I hope that a rethinking of civility might help us as individuals seek better versions of ourselves.

Regarding goals: I teach five processes with goals of fairness, awareness, harmony, compassion, and insight. The transformation I promise is both for you (the reader)—your creation and embodiment of civility in the place you live—and for our country—in that those who read and practice can evince it, or possibly transform it, improving on it, and thus shaping the theory and practice of civility presented here.

Regarding occasions: You are reading this book. I hope occasions are extended when you and other readers share it—and your experience of it—with still others. Perhaps it will serve as a guide for groups who want to take up the study of civility. It might serve as a text in courses at various post-secondary levels.[9] Civics courses are not often taught in high schools, but it could work in courses on American government, often offered at the senior level. Or perhaps students might form civility clubs to enact the principles laid out here for causes linked to their school, neighborhood, or, more expansively the current civic issues that need most attention.

Regarding timing: the "make America great again" trope is in the air. This book is a discussion around the trope—the nature of America's greatness, especially as civility plays a role is establishing that greatness. Put more modestly, this book suggests what individuals as citizens might contribute to making America strong and kind. To repeat myself for purposes of making a point about rhetorical analysis, I believe citizens can breathe new life into civility, the new, robust sort I describe herein, through civility activism. That activism will necessarily derive from you making the content of this book your own.

On a personal level, retirement has provided me the opportunity to write, and the pleasure and hard work of exploring a subject I care about. My writing has been a learning process and a scholarly adventure. I knew I wanted to think and write on civility, a word that floats around in my memory of growing up. What I have produced, no surprise, draws not only on my research but also on major themes in my personal and professional life.

Regarding exigence: What compels me to enter now? My responses above point to an answer: I wish to pass on to the world my ideas for creating a new civility.

To complicate the situation, if you wish, you, too, as reader/listener, can figure out comparable examples as you proceed, for in reading, you too are in the act of creation, of constructing a situation, of emergent meaning-making. You know why you are reading and can understand its impact by thinking through the elements of our model as they operate in your life.

Notice how the list below complicates the dynamics of civility. I will
not explicate but I will ask you (as reader) to consider how I (as writer)
handled constraints in my reasoning, and how, as part of emerging meaning-making, you respond. The rhetorical situation continually evolves.
The constraints are listed here:

- The explanations or evidence I employed;

- What I emphasized, left out, or downplayed;

- What kind of language I used;

- What I imagined about the nature and disposition of the
  audience;

- In a larger sense, what I thought about the state of affairs, or
  the state of the world beyond the specific issue at hand; and,
  finally,

- Who else has said something that is worth weaving into my
  own analysis?

I thought about each and every one of these constraints as I wrote. (An
implicit knowing about all that needs to be addressed is what makes the
writing task often seem daunting.) One of the satisfactions of reading is
that you (as reader) can bring your implicit knowing to the meaning I am
making, thus advancing the quality of the text.

We can think of contingencies as part of constraints. Some of them
are beyond my control. The meaning you make of *Creating a New Civility* is
contingent on what you bring to your reading of it. I am trying to shape
those contingencies. Part of the work of social and political activists is to
point out the contingencies at play in a situation, for example, in the dis-
proportionate number of black people who are stopped for traffic cita-
tions, creating a need for black parents to give their black children "the
Talk." We can look for those contingencies in what activists call the inter-
sections between say, race and class, or gender and class. At play is who
holds power and how they hold it, as we learned in our section on politics
in our identity interrogation.

To review, we are here focusing on situations. We have visualized the
rhetorical/communication situation as a triangle: I, you, and it, each on a
point of a triangle, simultaneously interacting, with contexts and con-

straints that affect our conversation. As such, the rhetorical situation continually evolves. I make, for example, a comment about President Trump that you disagree with, and the situation alters. Perhaps you soak my comment in, continue reading, thinking about it as you go, or you find it so egregious that you put the book down—if so, not forever, but only to catch your breath until you can take the comment in and come to terms with it.

It is amazing how in everyday situations, through observation and practice, we figure the dynamics out naturally as a conversation (even an argument) rolls along. Yet when the situation is unfamiliar and when we are seeking common ground—especially when we are facing adversity—it is helpful to retrieve from our civil minds all we know about the dynamics of a situation.

We are gaining clarity in understanding civility dynamics. Feels good, doesn't it? Hard work, yet where else but a rhetorical analysis can we deal with the complex dynamics involved in getting to common ground? Analyzing a rhetorical situation is where we start.

"Breathing-Into" Meditation

We need a break before we take up our second model. An interlude to absorb our lesson in reasoning. Let us indulge ourselves in a meditative coming to terms over what we have just reviewed, some centering reflection on our emerging sense of civility.

First of all, take some long deep breaths. On the intake, feel the breath move to your feet and, on the outbreath, feel your breath glide up through your body to your head, expelling it through your nose or slightly open mouth. More deep, long belly breaths. Long, deep in-breath. On the outbreath, air glides through your body, a "civility glide" that infuses the spirit of civility within it; breathing as if for the common good of those parts we named on your interior, the naming bringing them into consciousness, the naming acquired through the adventure of our five explorations now infused through your spirit. Breathe into each separately. Body. Heart. Mind. Soul. Now breathe into them as a whole, the bodyheartmindsoul totally integrated. So much richer and fuller than when we began our journey. Your breathing infuses your body with a common-good spirit, a free spirit.

Let us especially notice our mind. We know our mind to be self-organized, we feel our mind as embodied, we realize it as emergent. We breathe into it as relational. All this happening simultaneously. It feels right. Breathe into the wonder of our mind. The wonder that allows us to wrap our heads around the complexity and power of civility.

We are comfortable in this deep breathing process, our practice making it second nature, as if it were our civility nature. In this deep breathing, our civility spirit infuses our body. Breathe into our identity, as we understand it now—our identity transformation, our identity then and now, transformed as it is through the consciousness-raising of our five processes.

We are paying attention. Around us, a civility milieu. We create it through the resonance of our senses, and the careful, accountable way we listen. Breathe into standing-under listening, the very words we hear washing over us, allowing us to hear in a new way, in a way that senses the consciousness of others and empathizes with them. Bring the other into our caring consciousness and let them find a place there. Imagine ourselves engrossed in a philosophy of caring.

And now, in bringing your meditation to an end, breathe into your pure being, your essence, your intrinsic nature, the substance of which you consist, your full humanity. Then breathe into possibilities—for civility.

Reasoning with a Focus on Act

In our analysis above, we looked at the situation in play, considering the interactions of speaker and audience over a subject, within the context and constraints that impinge on the situation.

But suppose we want to get more specific. Suppose we want to directly address a particular act within those dynamics. Suppose we want to get at motive: The words we wish we could take back, the racial insult, the LGBTQ+ insult, the objectification and harassment of women, fewer cents on the dollar paid per hour to women and racial minorities for equivalent work, the slap from anger; the shot that kills. These are all different kinds of abuses: verbal, racial, gender-based, economic, domestic, and the abuse of the basic human right to not be killed.[10]

Suppose we want to look at acts on a smaller scale (relatively speaking), as in Colin Kaepernick's act of taking the knee in the fall football season

2017 as the national anthem was played, expressing his First Amendment right of protest; or on a larger scale, as the public, especially sports fans, respond to his protest, and as other football teams show unwillingness to hire him after his action, despite his superior skills.

Or the seemingly small act of bravery of Rosa Park's unwillingness in late 1955 to take a seat in the back of the bus; on a larger scale the role that act played in the civil rights movement. Or the Las Vegas Strip massacre in late 2017 when fifty-eight people were shot and eight hundred and fifty injured, leading to a debate among members of Congress, the NRA, and the American public. Or the school shooting in Parkland, Florida, where seventeen people were killed by a former student with an assault rifle and the gun control protests that grew from that massacre.

As part of our understanding of civility dynamics, we want a framework for thinking through the implications of acts themselves as part of (in)civility dynamics.

A distinguished rhetorician can help us with this task—Kenneth Burke. Recall we drew on his definition of rhetoric earlier and on his concept of consubstantiation—being with in substance. A big word, connoting comfort, as in I am with you in my being, in my wholeness. I return to this big word because of the potential of consubstantiation as a foundation for civility. I would imagine Burke imagined countries in consubstantiation, being with in substance, in a harmonious way of life.

Burke's ultimate goal was peacemaking. In 1945, just after the scourge of Nazism in WWII, he wanted to write "a response to theories of human motivation based on psychological, sociological, and scientific [thinking] that [he] felt did not encompass the full complexity of the human situation."[11] He developed that response in *Grammar of Motives*. (Think of grammar here in the larger sense of relationships between words in use, not in the more common sense of rules and usage.) Ambitious, yes? As we are here.

In *Grammar*, Burke developed "a philosophy of language and human relationships" that he called Dramatism, illustrated in the graphic. His use of dramatism rather than the simpler drama indicates he is thinking big, theorizing a way to think about human relations and solutions to injustices.

He writes, "If action, then drama; if drama, then conflict; if conflict, then victimization. . . . Dramatism [is always] on the edge of this vexing problem.... [And man] is the kind of being that is particularly distinguished by an aptitude for such action."[12] It is my hope that, through *Creating a New Civility*, we might alter Burke's conclusion to "... if conflict, then the possibility of civility." We too are interested in motives for peace: an alternative way to conceptualize civility—actions in the name of peace.

Burke was interested in motivations, and following that, the acts that come from them. Burke opens his introduction by asking: "What is involved, when we [ask] what people are doing and why they are doing it?" The following graphic makes Burke's conceptualization ever so much more easily understood. I suggest you refer to it as our discussion proceeds. As our illustration shows, these terms are typically presented in the shape of a pentad. For him, the focus in relationships is on acts first and foremost. Burke called out five key terms as "the generating principles of his investigation." The conceptualization is sometimes referred to as Burke's Pentad but I will also refer to it with Burke's name for it—"Dramatism," as the latter term connotes the drama in the act that is at the heart of our analysis.

Hence, the term act appears at the top of the pentad. His primary terms, shown above as the five points of the pentad, are:

- Act—"what took place, in thought or deed";

- Scene—"what was the background of the act, the situation in which it occurred";

- Agent—"what person or kind of person performed the act";

- Agency—"what means or instruments [were] used"; and

- Purpose—"why, what was the motive?"

As to why he chose these particular terms, Burke explains that they "are understandable at a glance." He writes:

> ... the terms are always there for us to reclaim, in their everyday simplicity, their almost miraculous easiness, [they enable] us constantly to begin afresh. When they might become difficult, when we can hardly see them, through having stared at them too intensely, we can [all] of a sudden relax, to look at them as we always have, lightly, glancingly. And having reassured ourselves, we can start out again, once more daring to let them look strange and difficult.[13]

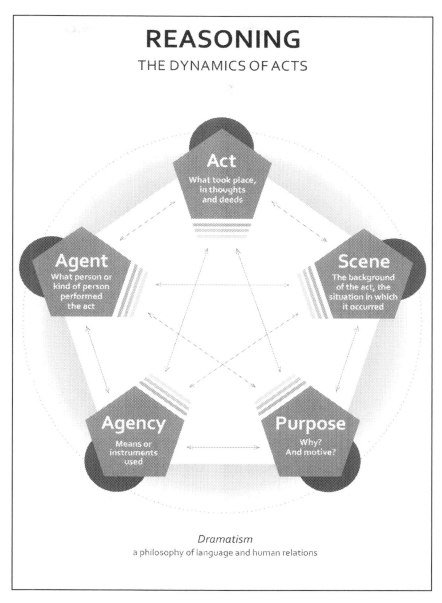

REASONING
THE DYNAMICS OF ACTS

Act
What took place,
in thoughts
and deeds

Agent
What person or
kind of person
performed
the act

Scene
The background
of the act; the
situation in which
it occurred

Agency
Means or
instruments
used

Purpose
Why?
And motive?

Dramatism
a philosophy of language and human relations

Illustration by Susan Panning.

We will use Burke's Pentad as our way to analyze acts in our search for civility. Understandable and familiar, the terms are available for rich analysis of situational dynamics. Basically, Burke is interested, as we are, not only in the Pentad points as such but also in the relationships among them. His "dramatism" looks at those relationship and asks "Why?" (You may recognize the pentad's points as the journalist's who, what, where, when, how, and why questions.)

Burke named these relationships among the terms; he called them *ratios*. We have ten ratios to help us unravel the complexities in any act. Follow the arrows on our graphic and work clockwise around the pentad. The first five ratios between each of the primary terms are represented by exterior arrows connecting the outer terms of the Pentad:

Act—Scene,
Scene—Purpose,
Purpose—Agency,
Agency—Agent,
Agent—Act,

and the last five ratios, (represented by interior arrows on the diagram),

Act—Purpose,
Act—Agency,
Agent—Scene,
Agent—Purpose, and
Agency—Scene.

The very construction of the Pentad shows the dynamism of the relationships. It would wise for you to spend a minute or so studying each of the terms themselves, and the ratios, or the ten relationships among them. We will discuss the five terms, recognizing their natural folding into one another, moving clockwise around the pentad.

Act is the pivotal term at the top of the diagram. Imagine an act as a simultaneous coming-together of all five of the terms, and all ten ratios. As you review the terms themselves, and then the ratios, you see that the process of identifying them is generative in and of itself. In fleshing them out, we get a full picture of an act—the facts, the history, the complexity. Note that Burke was particularly interested in two incredibly important ratios—why did the act take place (in thought or deed), and how? As we did in our focus on situations above, we will walk through an example of how this works in practice. Try to apply what you learned above to what emerges here in Burke's analysis of acts.

Analyzing an Act of Voting with Burke's Pentad, aka Dramatism

To get a feel for how we might use dramatism to help get to truth in civil situations, let us use the example of you exercising the right to vote in the next presidential election. I like the idea of framing your act of voting as drama, as analyzing the situation tells a story, your story of how you come to vote the way you will. In calling out the terms and the ratios, the approach takes you and your reasoning seriously and reckons with the way each term influences your act. Again, you are establishing a vocabulary to talk about the particulars of reasoning, looking to the role it plays in civil actions. Our examples clarify and pull no punches, presenting reasoning as they do in all its complexity.

I also like the idea of working with a vote, as it has such strong symbolic meaning in our effort after civility. It is the single most powerful form that every citizen has to connect with decision-makers in our legislatures— local, state, and national—to communicate their desires to those who hold power and to impact their decision-making. In that sense, voting is the most powerful civility action you possess, your most basic act in the practice of freedom.

It is appropriate to explore the dramatism in your vote for the next president, as there will be drama in making your choice, thinking it through, talking it over, listening to dialogue wherever you are, through many mediums.

Refer to the graphic as we proceed, starting with scene because that is where your act will occur.

Regarding scene: There is first and foremost the voting booth itself, the cubicle where your voting act is carried out. But there is also a larger setting that radiates from the local to the national. It has been said that the 2016 election made the "all politics is local" saying quaint, in that identity affiliation proved more powerful than grassroots party affiliation. On the other hand, sometimes issues set grassroots activism in motion, as when the Florida high school shooting sent student activists and their supportive communities to the White House and Congress. (In the long term such activism can play a significant role.)

You are aware if and how your voting district has been gerrymandered—perhaps along partisan or racial lines—in an effort to deliver district votes to a certain party. A look at the map of gerrymandering in the United Sates tells the sad story of the politicization of our very vote through the partisan rigging of elections. A recent Supreme Court decision means the issue of partisan redistricting will be left to the states. Indeed very recently, a North Carolina state court ruled that its legislative district map is unconstitutional in that it reflects "extreme partisan gerrymandering," a decision that could very well impact other states. Congress also has a hand. It may first end gerrymandering with the Redistricting Reform Act of 2019 (H.R.3572), which, as I write, is in the House Committee on the Judiciary for deliberation.[14] As an informed voter, you will want to learn how this issue is resolved.

There is also the issue of whether the voting machine itself has been rigged, and if and how the ballots will be managed accountably. You have followed stories about presidential elections as a security issue and about how vulnerable our election system is to hacking. You have not fallen victim to propaganda and disinformation promulgated by hackers using fake social media accounts or bots to influence a community's thinking.

In any case, you as agent arrive at the scene—the designated voting place in your neighborhood. You intend to vote. You check in with a volunteer to confirm that you are registered, show proof of your identity, receive a ballot, and enter a booth—a process, we must note, that is much easier for some in this country than for others, a historically discriminative process for black people and minorities, a process compromised by gerrymandering, and, most recently, by lame-duck legislation to limit the power of newly elected, incoming legislators. It is just the beginning and the act has been complicated by the dynamics (or in Burke's term, the drama) in act and scene. You act. You vote for the person you think best qualified for the presidency. You are exercising a basic right of freedom, one of your most sacred acts of civility. A good deal of thought has gone into preparing for this very act. Perhaps you have worked in the run-up to the election to get voters registered. If so, you are aware of the constraints on voting privilege, your own and others. Constraints such as voter ID laws, the elimination or limitation of early voting options, of voting hours, and of sites that allow access to the privileged and deny it to those who work long hours, or have health or transportation challenges. America's political parties have a sorry history of manipulation of all of the above to deny the privilege to vote.

We assume you are eligible to vote. You have the privilege of the ballot, which in terms of Burke's Dramatism, is your agency. (Recall that Burke is most interested in the act-agency and act-purpose relationships.) You can also think of the ballot as a critical agency of civility in and of itself, knowing as we do that civility lives and breathes, just as we do. In voting, you are practicing freedom. In voting, in making your choice, your identity—all those markers of Exploration #1—come into play. You have studied the candidates and the issues. Altogether, the consciousness-raising of our first four processes helps you to an intelligent decision that serves civility well.

What do you as agent bring to the voting booth, the scene, and to the act? Hopefully, common-good interests. You have thought carefully about your vote; talked, even argued about it with family, friends and colleagues; followed news reports in respected venues, careful to think through their credibility, be they newspaper, television, or electronic. You've considered the stature of the journalists themselves, and their body of work in reporting the news. You are aware of how biases shape reports, reporters, and the institutions within which they work, and how your own (un)conscious biases may be interpreting them.

You are aware of the important role of the journalistic function, protected by the First Amendment, so significant it is called the fourth estate, in that its function is a counterbalance to the three branches of government themselves even as it is separate from each of them.

You have guarded against the possibility that propaganda or disinformation could have influenced your decision-making.

You as agent, and the scene in which you vote—each has a history, small in the moment, but large in how the moment came to be and in how your civil life is lived.

Regarding purpose: you are exercising a basic right, taking on the responsibility of citizenship. Your vote may be for, or against, as some voters reported in the last election—not so much for Donald Trump himself but rather against Hillary Clinton, or vice versa. Perhaps you support a particular party, so dedicated that you vote the ticket, rather than looking for the better candidate. We vote the way we do for many reasons, some that go to how we were reared and others to, say, our age in that life experience often changes our political perspective.

As a way to center yourself for this responsibility, look at the relationship between act and purpose. You ask yourself—long before you approach the scene, but most certainly then—Why am I voting the way I intend to? What are my motives? They will be complex: they will attend to your life so far, how you came to be liberal or conservative; the reading and people who inform your thinking; your life circumstances, situations, and jobs you have held that gave you insight; whatever else that contributes to the meaning-making behind this decision.

There is much more to be said about each of the terms and ratios, far more than we tap here, and which you can write about in your civility journal and talk about in your civility circles. The potential of the Pentad is in the power within and among its terms. Given our examples, why not think through how they might play out in your vote in the coming election? Why will you vote the way you do? As a starting point, be grateful for your agency—that encompasses your very right to vote. Deny people their agency and you deny their personhood, their freedom, a fact known only too well by women and people of color.

Even from our initial scan of Burke's Pentad, we realize the depths to be plumbed in each of the terms. Burke thought of the exercise we just completed as a way to look at the "grammar" behind a motive, as a way to understand an act. As you can see, the pentad terms, with the ratios interacting altogether, and always consistently in that they are always there to be considered, offer a way to understand the dynamism of any situation. As they are especially good for complex, value-ridden, contentious situations, they are suited for analysis of politics.

Knowing either model—Bitzer's "The Rhetorical Situation" with its three points of interaction, or Burke's "Dramatism," with its five points, or a combined focus on both situation and act—you can reason your way through complex situations and trust the decisions that result.

Reason is the magic of these approaches. No sleight of hand. Just the facts. You'll need practice, enough so that the dynamic relationships in these models becomes second nature. You need the entirety of either model for rich reasoning, for making meaning that informs judgment.

In fact, our approach via the models has a name. Either model might be called a heuristic, a method for getting to a solution of a problem or to the understanding of a contentious situation, a method that is systematic enough to be somewhere between a random approach (to be avoided) and a recipe (no such animal in discourse, because, as we know, drama is always present).

Our philosopher Kenneth Burke would have us think of how we might act together. We turn to him in conclusion.

A Doctrine of Consubstantiation

In thinking again of our ultimate goal of creating and sustaining civility, how does Kenneth Burke help us see it and bring it to fruition?

Recalling the culmination of our caring flow of Process #4, compassion, remember too that Burke saw consubstantiation not only as a goal, but also as the processes of understanding that overlap and that makes us substantially alike. Recall also that Burke's use of the term is different from that employed in religious doctrine. Burke explains (notice his focus, as always, on acts):

> A doctrine of *consubstantiality*, either explicit or implicit, may be necessary to any way of life. For *substance*, in the old philosophies, was an act, and a way of life is an *acting-together*; and in acting together, people have common sensations, concepts, images, ideas, attitudes that make them *consubstantial*.[15] (italics belong to Burke)

Let us dwell for a minute on Burke's use of substance as an act, a way of acting together in order to induce cooperation. In creating civility, we look at our substance, in the full and rich sense that Burke conceptualizes it, as a way of acting together. Devoted to the philosophy of process as we are, we can get to substance if we look at processes of living and acting together, as we have done here. It is the substance of civility that will take us there.

I would not be giving you a fair analysis of Burke's thinking about consubstantiality if I failed to mention his concern for victimization, or scapegoating, as he also referred to the irrational hostilities that can develop in a like-minded group. I have confidence, though, that the four processes that precede our discussion of reasoning counteract the scapegoating tendency—to the extent that any reasonable course of action can.

In Burke's terms, through *Creating a New Civility* we are creating an *epistemology*, a study of the nature and grounds of knowledge, for "acting-together," with what he would call a "God-term,"[16] of civility; in Burke's thinking, civility itself would describe a fundamental ground for civil action, as the term God does for religious epistemologies.

I like to think that *Creating a New Civility*, as it describes a way of coming together, will play a pivotal role in Americans acting together in consubstantiation.

Here is our resolution, as Earth citizens, for the new millennium: may civility become a way of life; let civil acts fold into the here-and-now, moment-by-moment of our living.

Toward Common Good

What is it we hold in our hands?

A book about civility. In its early pages, we held a graphic of our hands holding civility, our fingers already feeling the processes we would undertake, reaching for our goals. We have used a hands-on process, pardon the pun, so that we might touch others with civility.

The effort has been personal. My narratives tell you of my life.

The topic of civility came to me as a calling. I said to twin sister Judy, as if pulling an idea out of the blue, "I want to write a book on civility." The possibility had not come to me before, and here it was in front of me, full blown.

Knowing that our conversations hadn't touched civility, she replied, "You'd better get a library card." Bless her. Not, "Don't try something like that! The subject is impossible." Instead, an unstated "I believe in you. Let's see what you come up with." A respect for a "calling" was part of our heritage. Our Uncle Walter had been called to the ministry, and our maternal grandfather to Christianity.

I understand now that I thought of civility under the guise of peacefulness, a coming to terms about how to live with less stress, in a place where parity exists, where space is shared, where events of life are not always an encounter, where there is evenness and openness and lovingkindness. Simultaneously, finding myself among all that, answering the question, "Who am I, given the experiences of my seventy-some years?" I hope for you a similar "coming to terms."

I spent a year reading about civility and taking notes. I found that civility has its own parameters. I liked thinking big about culture and society, accustomed to doing so through my training in American Studies, which also accustomed me to the complex reasoning and dry language of scholarly theory. I identified differences in point of view, understanding the various approaches that each scholar brought to the larger body of knowledge.

What could I add to the civility discussion?

My approach was intuitive yet born of experience. My previous scholarship had, theoretically, done similar work: describing and analyzing good practices, in the first case in Louisa May Alcott's short stories for little girls and in the second, along with my co-author, in writing program administration.

What good practices might I discover for living a life replete with civility?

I began, coffee first, then mindfulness meditation, a bit of reading—an essay, a poem or two, passages in the mindfulness literature. Then down the stairs to my desk, where I found inspiration in the beauty of Summit County Metropolitan Park.

I committed myself to the philosophy of process, to the philosophy of becoming—I would write my way to the understanding and practice of civility.

I began by posing the identity question "Who am I?" (as I was also doing in my mindfulness group study). I identified ten identity markers, four of which I have explored here. How do gender, race, religion, and politics mark me, mark us all? What questions must we ask of ourselves to interrogate our prejudices as well as our contributions in order to arrive at fairness for all? What would our personal and public landscapes look like when we asked those questions of ourselves?

I examined myself as I understood myself, as body + heart + mind + soul. How might I understand the space that was me? Mindfulness meditation showed a way. It followed logically to examine the space around us, taking up our perceptions, especially the one sense we don't engage fully—listening. What dynamism goes on when we really hear what is said in order to respond genuinely and accountably?

Relationships with others underpinned the first three processes; in the fourth I would bring them front and center. What would characterize a caring relationship? How might I best relate to others? What would doing so feel like? How would I act? What would I do?

Finally, how would I manage the language and reasoning behind this abundance of knowledge in sorting through the complexities of (un)civil acts and situations?

I would define a way of being in civility, a theory and practice of civility, something within humanity's reach. I found my way to relevant scholarship and the thinking of fine minds.

A focus on process would be appropriate for such a goal, as life is constantly changing, as people who lead us change, as wars rage on, as rogue killings of all kinds continue, and as all of us still long for peaceful coexistence. The process continues as you write your civility story, looking for fairness, awareness, harmony, compassion, and insight.

I collected definitions. Adam McClellan's concepts of full humanity, interdependence of us all, and common cause suggested what I was wanting to show—a new civility for our times, one that he insisted, as I would, that no group ever be relegated to a second-class or lesser status, or that privileged principles would be prized over human beings. I decided to call it a new civility to differentiate from past uses of civility that assign inferiority.

The incivilities I saw at all levels in public life prompted me to keep going, as did my desire for personal equanimity. Judy saw all the drafts, and her insights forced clarification. It was Judy, with her empathetic mindset from hundreds of conversations, who saw an emerging framework and helped me coax it onto paper.

Now I leaf through my definitions, once again reviewing the Post-its in my books, looking at what I had underlined, seeing it anew.

Does the description of how civility might be manifested capture, for example, what Edward Shils believed civility to be? His collected essays hold this title: *The Virtue of Civility*. He conceptualizes civility as a behavior showing high moral standards. He believes we might hold an idea of such behavior in "an inclusive collective self-consciousness." Have we met Shils on his ground?

We reach for inclusiveness, abhorring racism, gender inequities, partisanship, and an evangelism born of any of the above. Our practice is collective—five processes, drawing on relevant scholars, bringing our "sub-stances," (recall Kenneth Burke's consubstantiation) and our ways of being and seeing ourselves, into equilibrium with others through listening, caring and reasoning. Collective in addressing how (in)civility resides in race, gender identity, religion, and politics; collective in that we examined five aspects of our being; collective in our focus on interdependence of us all; collective in our focus on the personal and the public, at all levels of our life—local, state, national, world. Our civility consciousness is writ large. We attempt to hold the knowledge of ourselves and our realms of being within our totality. We aim for that totality to be one with the universe.

Shils asks that we give precedence to an "inclusive collective self-con-sciousness" over our individual consciousness that too often resides in self-centeredness. Indeed, we have. Yet we must hold on to our sense of self while giving precedence to the greater good—what our new civility is all about.

Robert Reich describes the common good in his book of the same title:

> The common good . . . is a set of shared commitments to the rule of law, and to the spirit as well as the letter of the law; to our democratic institutions of government; to truth; to tolerance of our differences; to equal political rights and equal opportunity; to participating in our civic life, and making necessary sacrifices for the ideals we hold in common.
>
> We must share these commitments if we are to have a functioning society. They inform our judgments about right and wrong because they constitute our common good. Without them, there is no "we."[1]

Now, at the end of our journey, we project civility charisma, because we know civility from the inside out. We (try to) manifest it in our very being, civility always an ongoing enterprise.

The discussions of civility I read in preparing for this book were invariably placed in a larger societal perspective. Let us look large as we conclude. Let us return to our founding document, our Constitution and examine its Preamble, realizing, as we read through the lens of civility what is already familiar:

> We the People of the United States, in Order to form a more perfect Union, establish Justice, insure domestic Tranquility, provide for the common Defence, promote the general Welfare, and secure the Blessings of Liberty to ourselves and our Posterity . . .

Creating a New Civility is our effort to breathe new life into that assertion.

Overall, the world is now a far better place to live, according to most any dimension we can measure, than it has been in the past. As Steven Pinker reminds us in his recent *Enlightenment Now*, we have reason, science, humanism, and progress on our side. Our new civility paradigm fits nicely alongside, contributing further to enlightenment.

Within the abundance of enlightenment are the eternal qualities of joy, wonder, and awe. We have seen them flicker in moments of listening and caring, even, paradoxically, in questioning and examining. Also in moments of insight, which we treasure in memory. Reflection tells us those moments have transported us to a state of grace. Put more simply, creating a new civility makes us happy because our humanity is being fulfilled. In those moments we experience full humanity.

Our civility consciousness urges us to connect, as my father always did, by looking another in the eye, smiling, saying hello, extending a hand, and asking, "How's the world treating you?" I like his global image and the range of responses his question inspires. I like its unstated counterpart: how are you treating the world?

The idea of how I treat the world has always been with me. When I asked my mother what I should be when I grew up, she would say, "Whatever you do, find a way to make the world a better place."

The impulse to civility has always been with me. Giving life to the impulse has been healing for me.

Hard as the effort toward civility is, there is, in its commitment to others, in its examination of how we connect to them, a profound possibility—that civility heals, that the Earth's "inclusive collective consciousness," can heal, one civil action at a time.

The book is now out of my hands. I hand it over with the mixed emotion I had when I sent my daughters off to college, thinking of the pleasure and pain I had in nurturing them, and hopeful for them in their next steps in life's journey. My hope is that the book's ideas will come to reside in the public consciousness.

Its centerpiece, the new civility paradigm, will be revised. New political, religious, sociological, economic, and environmental realities will emerge, and those who reside in civility will change its parameters to enhance a still newer civility. Such is how knowledge advances. The paradigm's particulars will accommodate to local, national, and global realities. That is the beauty of the paradigm. Its particulars are there to suggest strategic uses of civility.[2] What we learn will fold into the evolutionary process of creating a still newer paradigm. Its beauty is in its action—doing what we can, within our families, neighborhoods, communities, organizations, institutions, enterprises, and endeavors—to create common good.

Notes

Introduction

1. Cahoone, "Civic Meetings, Cultural Meanings," 47.

2. Edmundson, *Self and Soul.*

3. *Deep structure* is a theoretical concept defined by Noam Chomsky that linguists use to unify several related structures—a concept borrowed in architecture, music, politics—and now civility studies.

4. See my website for Lawrence E. Cahoone's definition of civility, from *Civil Society: The Conservative Meaning of Liberal Politics,* 212.

5. Brooks, "American Renewal."

Process #1

1. Altogether, I count ten markers that shape our identity: four are "defined" in utero—body/mind as described in DNA, gender, race, and time; three are shaped in our home environment—place, class, and ethnicity; and three are shaped as we mature—politics, religion, and education. The scope of this book does not allow examination of all ten. You can go to my website for a brief discussion of how all ten relate to civility identity. I focus here on four markers that are central to incivilities in today's society.

2. Coates, *Between the Word and Me,* 29.

3. Coates, *Between,* 29.

4. Coates, "Letter to My Son."

5. "Global village," as I use it here and throughout derives from Marshall McLuhan, who used the term in *The Gutenberg Galaxy* (1962) to refer to a world made small and without boundaries resulting from instantaneous communication from any one place to all other places simultaneously, through electronic communication. He wrote, "The new electronic interdependence recreates the world in an image of a global village." I remember both the fascination and reservation my fellow graduate students had about the concept as we studied McLuhan's text, reactions that still seem appropriate so many years later. Hillary Clinton capitalizes on the concept in *It Takes A Village*, in which she writes about a child's interdependence with many individuals, groups, and social and public institutions, which Clinton believes have responsibility in caring for a child.

6. *Gay Community Endowment Fund.* https://www.transakron.com/terminology.

7. *Merriam-Webster*, s.v. "gender (n.)," "gendered (n.)," http://www.merriam-webster .com/dictionary/app.

8. *Merriam-Webster*, s.v. "bias (n.)," "prejudice (n.)," http://www.merriam-webster.com /dictionary/app.

9. Barker. Letter re Senate Bill 2578 on 2020 census.

10. AAA Statement on Race.

11. Goodman and Darnovsky, and 31 other signatories. "Race, Genetics, and a Controversy."

12. Brief History of OMB Directive 15.

13. Swaine and McCarthy, "Young Black Men."

14. Schuessler, "Ibram X. Kendi Has a Cure for America's 'Metastatic Racism.'"

15. Kendi, "Heartbeat of Racism is Denial."

16. Kendi,"Heartbeat."

17. William R. Murry, *Reason and Reverence*, 10

18. Murry, 11

19. Murry, 11

20. Thiessen, "Krauthammer."

21. Levitsky and Ziblatt, "Democracies," 5.

22. Levitsky and Ziblatt, 23–25.

23. Levitsky and Ziblatt, 65–67.

24. Levitsky and Ziblatt, 37.

25. Levitsky and Ziblatt, 106.

26. *Merriam-Webster*, s.v. "politics" (n.), http://www.merriam-webster.com/dictionary /app.

27. To explore possibilities, consult the recent book by James Fallows and Deborah Fallows describing the exciting reforms in over two dozen communities—*Our Towns: A 100,000-Mile Journey into the Heart of America*. Inspiring.

28. To reflect on your commitment to creating civility, see my website for alternate ways to conceptualize the new civility.

Process #2

1. Kabat-Zinn, *Full Catastrophe Living*, 5.

2. Kabat-Zinn, 19.

3. See books co-authored by Mark Williams and Danny Penman, as well as Mark Williams, John Teasdale, Zindel Segal, and Jon Kabat-Zinn, cited in the bibliography.

4. Boyce, "Defining Mindfulness," 6.

5. Siegel, *Aware*, 29. Seigel's most recent book, *Aware*, delves into science-based practices of "cultivating consciousness by expanding awareness." He delves into the nature of energy, which takes him to physics, and physics-inspired insights about the nature of consciousness. Exciting—linking science with subjective experience!

6. Siegel, *Mind: A Journey to the Heart of Being Human*, 53.

7. Siegel, *Mind*, 53.

8. Siegel, *Mind*, 53.

9. Moffett, *The Universal Schoolhouse*, xix.

10. A wealth of information about mindfulness has been published in the last decade, including apps, to help one maintain calm in the face of crisis. I suggest that, as you work your way through this exploration, you visit a bookstore, and thumb your way through some of those many recent books. You may find an approach that appeals particularly to you and that will complement our study here. I found Dan Harris" *Meditation for Fidgety Skeptics*, which may be of interest if you worry that you may have troubling focusing. It's light-hearted, approachable, and full of examples, statistics, and his personal testimony to show how mindfulness works. I recommend any of the apps of Jon Kabat-Zinn and "Unwinding Anxiety," by Judson Brewer, who is now Acting Director of the recently formed Division of Mindfulness at the University of Massachusetts Medical School.

11. Gendlin, *Focusing*, 60–63.

12. I sometimes used the concept of felt sense in writing classes, in conjunction with freewriting, a technique I encouraged students to use to help them discover ideas, and once discovered, to further them. Thank you, Peter Elbow, a leader in the teaching of writing as process, as opposed to emphasizing only product.

13. You can undertake this civility journey alone, but the resonance of a community adds immensely to the experience. Further, the discipline of the group, with its patterns of activities, is reinforcing. A mindful aura pervades the room, and it seems to soak into the collective being. If a good class is not available, put your hands on the Williams and Penman book and work your way through it as a more detailed counterpart to what you find here. Or go to Jon Kabat-Zinn's website and find classes at www.mindfulnesscds.com. The activities laid out below can be adapted for your Civility Circle.

14. William James, in his classic *Principles of Psychology,* quoted in Canales, *A Tenth of a Second,* 5.

15. Attributed to Thomas Edison's chief laboratory engineer, in Canales, 5. Canales says, "By studying the tenth of a second. . . .[this book] reveals some of the key characteristics of the modern era and illuminates the work of some of the most important scientists and philosophers of modern times," 2.

16. This three-minute breathing exercise is adapted from Williams and Penman, *Mindfulness,* 182–83.

17. Williams and Penman, *Mindfulness,* 96.

18. Kabat-Zinn, "Body Scan Meditation," November 29, 2016, https://www.youtube .com/watch?v=_DTmGtznab4.

19. *Merriam-Webster,* s.v. "wonder (*n.*), http://www.merriam-webster.com/dictionary /app.

Process #3

1. Kabat-Zinn, *Coming,* 103.

2. *Merriam-Webster,* s.v. "perception (*n.*)," http://www.merriam-webster.com/dictionary /app.

3. Glenn, *Unspoken,* 9.

4. Glenn, 18.

5. Glenn, 31.

6. Martin Jay, quoted in Ratcliffe, *Rhetorical Listening,* 22.

7. Joy Arbor, "With Our Ears to the Ground," 218.

8. Arbor, 217–230.

9. Ratcliffe, "Defining Rhetorical Listening," in *Rhetorical Listening,"* 17–46.

10. Ratcliffe, "Rhetorical Listening," 205, 206, 207.

11. Ratcliffe, "Rhetorical Listening," 207.

Process #4

1. Jennifer Schuessler, "Ibram X. Kendi Has a Cure for America's 'Metastatic Racism'."

2. The first line of Willliam Wordsworth's poem is "The world is too much with us; late and soon,/Getting and spending, we lay waste our powers." A few lines later, he says: "For this, for everything, we are out of tune;/It moves us not." It is likely this poem came to mind because, in a large sense, our effort here is to be "moved" to be be *in* tune, or as we say here, in harmony with all that is around us, including with nature, as Wordsworth so passionately calls for here.

3. Mayeroff, *On Caring,* 87.

4. Mayeroff, 67–68.

5. Mayeroff, 87.

6. Mayeroff, 54.

7. Mayeroff, 55.

8. Mayeroff, 55.

9. When *Caring* first appeared I endured a multitude of criticisms for my use of the word "feminine." Why not "feminist"? I am a feminist certainly, and I believe that *Caring* fits into the theoretical category of relational feminism. But when I wrote *Caring* [1984], I did not know much about feminist theory. I was working my own way through a set of problems, and I chose "feminine" to direct attention to centuries of experience more typical of women than men. "Feminine" pointed to a mode of experience, not to an essential characteristic of women, and I wanted to make clear that men might also share this experience. I still [2003] believe that, if we want males to participate fully in caring, a change of experience is required, starting in childhood. Abstract attempts at reeducation probably will not work (p. xvi).

10. Noddings, *Caring*, 36.

11. Noddings, 33.

12. Noddings, 72.

13. Buber, quoted in Noddings, *Caring*, 73.

14. Noddings, *Caring*, 74.

15. Glenn, citing Kenneth Burke, "Witnessing Silence," *Unspoken*, 49.

16. Shea, "Our Tribal Nature," Shea and Fiorina, eds., *Rude, Nasty Stubborn Politics*, 96.

17. Coates, *Eight Years in Power*, 186.

18. Coates, "Opening Statement," HR.40 Testimony on Reparations. June 19, 2019, amp.theatlantic.com.

19. Coates, *Eight Years in Power*, 207.

20. Mayeroff, *On Caring*, 54

Process #5

1. Covino and Jolliffe, eds. *Rhetoric*, 4.

2. Kenneth Burke, "A Rhetoric of Motives," 1032.

3. Weaver, "Language is Sermonic," 1044.

4. Aristotle, *Rhetoric*, in Bizzell and Herzberg, eds., 153.

5. Aristotle, 144.

6. Aristotle, 146.

7. I taught my students the I-You-It-C-C mnemonic before I sent them off to write essays of persuasion, even suggesting they write the mnemonic on their fingertips as a way of remembering it. You too can use the mnemonic when you are in conten-

tious situations to think through how "content" is being shaped in the discussion, in which case you will be conducting a rudimentary rhetorical analysis.

8. Bitzer, "The Rhetorical Situation," *Philosophy and Rhetoric*, 1, no.1 (January 1968), 1–14.

9. The course would include supplementary readings, drawn from those listed in the bibliography. Intriguing activities would include, for example, journal-keeping; the student's own civility narrative; an identity self-study of gender, race, religious, and political heritage; accounts of some feet-to-the-fire and standing-under listening; and, using the civility paradigm as a framework for understanding, writing blogs and analyses of local and national happenings.

10. I take the concept of non-killing from Glenn Paige, Former Director of the Peace Program at the University of Hawai'i, who thought even more basically than a desire for peace. He worked toward establishing non-killing as fundamental to a civil way of being.

11. Covino and Jolliffe, eds. "Dramatism." *Rhetoric*, 46.

12. Bizzell and Herzberg, eds. *The Rhetorical Tradition*, 1041.

13. Burke, in Bizzell and Herzberg, eds., *The Rhetorical Tradition*, 992.

14. Reform Act of 2019, https://www.govtrack.us/Redistricting.

15. Burke, in Bizzell and Herzberg, eds., 1020.

16. Bizzell and Herzberg, eds., 990.

Toward Common Good

1. Robert B. Reich, *The Common Good*, 182–83.

2. Susan Herbst, "The Powerful—If Elusive Nature of Civility," 17–26.

Bibliography

For a list of works for further research, go to www.civilitydynamics.com.

American Anthropological Association. "A Brief History of OMB Directive 15," 1997.https://www.learner.org/workshops/primarysources/census/docs/ombd.html.

American Anthropological Association. "Statement on Race," adopted May 17, 1998. https://www.americananthro.org/ConnectWithAAA/Content.aspx?ItemNumber=2583.

Alexander, Jeffrey C. *The Civil Sphere.* Oxford: Oxford University Press, 2006.

Arbor, Joy. "With Our Ears to the Ground: Compassionate Listening in Israel/Palestine." In *Silence and Listening as Rhetorical Acts,* edited by Cheryl Glenn and Krista Ratcliffe, 217–230. Carbondale: Southern Illinois University Press, 2011.

Aristotle. Passages on "Ethos, Logos, and Pathos" from *Rhetoric: Books I and II.* Ca 367–347 and 335–323 BCE. In *The Rhetorical Tradition: Readings from Classical Times to the Present,* edited by Bizzell and Herzberg, 151–160. Boston: Bedford Books of St. Martin's Press, 1990.

Barker, Alex. "AAA Letter in Support of the 2020 Census IDEA Act," https://www.americananthro.org/ParticipateAndAdvocate/AdvocacyDetail.aspx?ItemNumber=22922.

Bitzer, Lloyd. "The Rhetorical Situation." *Philosophy and Rhetoric* 1, no. 1, (January 1968), 1–14.

Bizzell, Patricia and Bruce Herzberg, eds. *The Rhetorical Tradition: Readings from Classical Times to the Present.* Boston: Bedford Books of St. Martin's Press, 1990.

Boyce, Barry. "Defining Mindfulness." *Mindful,* August 2018.

Brooks, David. "American Renewal," Opinion, *New York Times,* July 26, 2018.

Burke, Kenneth. Passages from *A Rhetoric of Motives*, 1950. In *The Rhetorical Tradition: Readings from Classical Times to the Present*, edited by Bizzell and Herzberg, 989–1041, Boston: Bedford Books of St. Martin's Press, 1990.

Cahoone, Lawrence E. *Civil Society: The Conservative Meaning of Liberal Politics*. Malden, MA: Blackwell Publishers, 2002.

Cahoone, Lawrence E. "Civic Meetings, Cultural Meanings." In *Civility*, edited by LeRoy S. Rouner, Notre Dame, Indiana: University of Notre Dame Press, 2000.

Cain, Susan. *Quiet: The Power of Introverts in a World that Can't Stop Talking*. New York: Crown Paperbacks, 2012.

Cameron, Julia. *The Artist's Way: A Spiritual Path to Higher Creativity*. New York: Penguin Random House, 2018.

Canales, Jimena. *A Tenth of a Second: A History*. Chicago: The University of Chicago Press, 2009.

Chemerinsky, Erwin. *We the People: A Progressive Reading of the Constitution for the Twenty-First Century*. New York: Picador/Macmillan, 2018.

Coates, Ta-Nehisi. *Between the World and Me*. New York: Spiegel and Grau, 2015.

Coates, Ta-Nehisi. "A Letter to My Son, "*Atlantic*, July 4, 2015. https://www .theatlantic.com/politics/archive/2015/07/tanehisi-coates-between-the-world -and-me/397619/.

Coates, Ta-Nehisi. *We Were Eight Years in Power: An American Tragedy*. New York: One World Publishing, 2017.

Covey, Stephen R. *The 7 Habits of Highly Effective People: Powerful Lessons in Personal Change*. New York: Simon & Schuster, 2013.

Covino, William A. and David A. Jollife. *Rhetoric: Concepts, Definitions, and Boundaries*. Boston: Allyn and Bacon, 1995.

Daly, Mary. *Gyn/Ecology: The Metaethics of Radical Feminism*. Beacon Press, 1990.

DiAngelo, Robin. *White Fragility: Why It's So Hard for White People to Talk About Racism*. Boston: Beacon Press, 2018.

Edmundson, Mark. *Self and Soul: A Defense of Ideals*. Cambridge, MA: Harvard University Press, 2015.

Freire, Paulo. *Pedagogy of the Oppressed*. Translated by Myra Bergman Ramos. New York: Continuum, 1986.

Gendlin, Eugene T. *Focusing*. New York: Guilford Press, 1996.

Glenn, Cheryl. *Unspoken: A Rhetoric of Silence*. Carbondale: Southern Illinois University Press, 2004.

Glenn, Cheryl and Krista Ratcliffe. *Silence and Listening as Rhetorical Arts*. Carbondale and Edwardsville: Southern Illinois University Press, 2011.

Goodman, Alan and Marcy Darnovsky. "Race, Genetics, and a Controversy." Letter to the editor. *New York Times*, April 2, 2018.

Harris, Dan, and Jeff Warren with Carlye Adler. *Meditation for Fidgety Skeptics: A 10% Happier How-to Book*. New York: Spiegel & Grau, 2018.

Herbst, Susan. "The Powerful—if Elusive—Nature of Civility." In *Can We Talk: The Rise of Rude, Hasty, Stubborn Politics*, edited by Daniel M. Shea and Morris P. Fiorina, New York: Pearson, 2013.

Ie, Amanda, Christelle T. Ngoumen, and Ellen J. Langer, eds. *The Wiley Blackwell Handbook of Mindfulness*. 2 vols. Malden, MA: Wiley Blackwell, 2014.

Kabat-Zinn, Jon. *Meditation Is Not What You Think: Mindfulness and Why It Is So Important*. New York: Hachette Books, 2018.

Kabat-Zinn, Jon. *Full Catastrophe Living: Using the Wisdom of Your Body and Mind to Face Stress, Pain, and Illness*. New York: Delta Trade Paperbacks, 2009.

Kabat-Zinn, Jon. Mindfulness App. https://www.mindfulnessapps.com.

Kendi, Ibram X. *Stamped from the Beginning: The Definitive History of Racist Ideas in America*. New York: Hachette Book Group, 2016.

Kendi, Ibram X. "The Heartbeat of Racism is Denial." Op-Ed piece. *New York Times Online*, January 13, 2018.

Levitsky, Steven and Daniel Ziblatt. *How Democracies Die*. New York: Crown, 2018.

Mayeroff, Milton. *On Caring*. New York: Perennial Library, Harper & Row, 1971.

McClellan, Adam. "Beyond Courtesy: Redefining Civility." In *Civility*, edited by LeRoy S. Rouner. Notre Dame, Indiana: University of Notre Dame Press, 2000.

Middleton, Joyce. "Finding Democracy in Our Argument Culture: Listening to Spike Lee's Jazz Funeral on the Levees." In *Silence and Listening as Rhetorical Acts*, edited by Cheryl Glenn and Krista Ratcliffe, 163–79. Carbondale: Southern Illinois University Press, 2011.

Moffett, James. "I, You, It." *College Composition and Communication*. Vol. 16, No. 5 (December 1965), 243–48.

Moffett, James. *The Universal Schoolhouse: Spiritual Awakening through Education*. San Francisco: Jossey-Bass, 1994.

Molloy, Michael. *Experiencing the World's Religions: Tradition, Challenge, and Change*. Seventh Edition. New York: McGraw-Hill, 2018.

Murry, William R. *Reason and Reverence: Religious Humanism for the 21st Century*. Boston: Skinner House Books, 2006.

Noddings, Nel. *Caring: A Feminine Approach to Ethics and Moral Education*. Second Edition, with a New Preface. Berkeley and Los Angeles: University of California Press, 2003.

O'Donohue, John. *Anam Cara: A Book of Celtic Wisdom*. New York: Harper Collins, Reprinted Perennial, 2004.

Obama, Barack. "Farewell Speech." Chicago, January 10, 2017.

Pinker, Steven. *Enlightenment Now: The Case for Reason, Science, Humanism, and Progress*. New York: Viking, 2018.

Rabinowitz, Peter. "Fictional Music: Toward a Theory of Listening." In *Theories of Reading, Looking, and Listening*, edited by Harry R. Garvin. East Brunswick, New Jersey: Associated UP, 1981: 193–206.

Reich, Robert B. *The Common Good*. New York: Alfred A. Knopf, 2018.

Ratcliffe, Krista. "Rhetorical Listening: A Trope for Interpretive Invention and a 'Code of Cross Cultural Conduct.'" *College Composition and Communication*, Vol. 51, No. 2 (December 1999): 195–224.

Ratcliffe, Krista. *Rhetorical Listening: Identification, Gender, Whiteness*. Carbondale: Southern Illinois University Press, 2005.

Rouner, LeRoy S., ed. *Civility*. Notre Dame, Indiana: University of Notre Dame Press, 2000.

Royster, Jacqueline Jones. "When the First Voice You Hear Is Not Your Own." *College Composition and Communication*, Vol. 47, No. 1 (February 1996): 29–40.

Schuessler, Jennifer. "Ibram X. Kendi Has a Cure for America's 'Metastatic Racism'." *New York Times* Online, 8/7/19.

Shea, Daniel. "Our Tribal Nature and the Rise of Nasty Politics." In *Can We Talk? The Rise of Rude, Nasty, Stubborn Politics*, edited by Daniel Shea and Morris Fiorina. New York: Pearson, 2013.

Shea, Daniel and Morris Fiorina, eds. *Can We Talk? The Rise of Rude, Nasty, Stubborn Politics*. New York: Pearson, 2013.

Shaull, Richard. "Foreword," Paulo Freire, *Pedagogy of the Oppressed*. Translated by Myra Bergman Ramos. New York: Continuum, 1986.

Shils, Edward. *The Virtue of Civility: Selected Essays on Liberalism, Tradition and Civil Society*. Edited by Steven Grosby. Indianapolis: Liberty Fund, 1997.

Siegel, Daniel J. *Aware: The Science and Practice of Presence, the Groundbreaking Meditation Practice*. New York: TarcherPerigee, 2018.

Siegel, Daniel J. *Mind: A Journey to the Heart of Being Human*. New York: W. W. Norton, 2017.

Siegel, Daniel J. and Madeleine W Siegel. "Thriving with Uncertainty." In *The Wiley Blackwell Handbook of Mindfulness*, Vol. I, edited by Amanda Ie, Christelle T. Ngoumen, and Ellen J. Langer. Malden MA: Wiley Blackwell, 2014.

Singer, Michael A. *The Untethered Soul: The Journey Beyond Yourself*. New Harbinger Publications/ Noetic Books; 2007.

Swaine, Jon and Ciara McCarthy. "Young Black Men Again Faced Highest Rate of US Police Killings in 2016." January 8, 2017. https://theguardian.com /us-news/2017/jan/08/the-counted-police-killings-2016-young-black-men.

Thiessen , Marc A. "What Krauthammer Taught Me." *Washington Post* Writers Group, in *Akron Beacon Journal*, June 14, 2018.

Weaver, Richard. "All Language is Sermonic." In *The Rhetorical Tradition: Readings from Classical Times to the Present*, edited by Bizzell and Herzberg, 1044–54, Boston: Bedford Books of St. Martin's Press, 1990.

Williams, Mark and Danny Penman. *Mindfulness: An Eight-Week Plan for Finding Peace in a Frantic World*. Foreword by Jon Kabat-Zinn. New York: Rodale, 2011.

Williams, Mark, John Teasdale, Zindel Segal, and Jon Kabat-Zinn. *The Mindful Way through Depression: Freeing Yourself from Chronic Unhappiness*. New York: The Guilford Press, 2007.

Yamada, Mitsuye. "Invisibility is an Unnatural Disaster: Reflections on Asian-American Women." *Bridge: An Asian American Perspective*, Vol. 7, No. 1: 11.

Photo: Laura Contant

World travel and fifteen homes in ten communities; a doctor-
ate in American Studies, a professorship in the University of
Hawai'i's Department of English, scholarship on Louisa May
Alcott, innovative teaching and administrative work, and the
good fortune to learn from students of diverse cultures; a
personal journey as Ohio farm girl, wife, mother, retiree,
and divorcée; an abiding love of books and nature—this lifetime of experiences fold into Joy Marsella's vision of a new
civility. Read more about her and find ways to create civility
at www.civilitydynamics.com.